Multi-Family Housing Management in Korea

Seong-Kyu Ha / Kwan-Ho Myong / Ah-Rim Ahn
Eun-Taek Kang / Ta-kwan Choi / Byung-Nam Park
Korea Research Institute of Housing Management

parkyoungsa

Preface

Multi-family housing accounted for 10.1% of total housing in South Korea(hereafter 'Korea') in 1980, which increased by about seven to eight times to 75.0% in 2017 over the last four decades. Very few countries have seen this kind of explosive growth in the number of households residing in multi-family housing within such a short period of time. In other words, Korea has experienced a rapid increase in multi-family housing in line with its economic growth-the so-called Miracle on the Han River-hence its nickname the "Republic of Apartments."

Multi-family housing has become established as a common type of residential housing in Korea. The course of this establishment was marked by a continuous series of wide-ranging issues regarding multi-family housing complexes, and as part of efforts to solve and prevent such issues, multi-family housing management systems were also developed on an ongoing basis. As a result, research findings indicate that residents of multi-family housing are more satisfied with their residence, relative to their counterparts living in detached housing.

Korea has placed efforts into continuously developing its multi-family housing management systems in three aspects. First, new laws were established to resolve problems with multi-family housing management, and amendments were made to existing laws in a bid to reflect reality. Second, the Korean government solidified its multi-housing management framework by introducing a housing manager qualification system, under which nationally-recognized experts are permitted to manage multi-family housing. Lastly, the government provided systematic education programs for occupants residing in multi-family housing, councils of occupants' representatives organized to decide important matters, and housing managers and housing management workers in charge of multi-family housing management. All these efforts led to creating an environment where multi-family housing is managed in a safe and efficient manner despite its rapid growth.

This book was published with an aim to introduce how multi-family housing management systems have developed in Korean society. Topics such as the development of New Towns, large-scale development projects of multi-family housing complexes, and redevelopment projects in Korea had already been introduced in Southeast Asia and other regions around the globe. However, this book appears to be the first that systemically addresses how to manage multi-family housing supplied in large quantities.

To this end, a group of authors including those working in relation to multi-family housing management and academics participated in the writing of this book. These authors include working-level experts of the Korea Housing Managers Association, a statutory body of housing managers, and research experts of the Korea Research Institute of Housing Management, which is responsible for conducting research on multi-family housing management on an ongoing basis. They focused on the background behind the increase in multi-family housing; the significance of multi-family housing management; multi-family housing management systems; the qualification system and expertise of housing mangers; management expenses, reserves for long-term repairs, and tasks of multi-family housing management systems; ways to vitalize communities; and the development directions of multi-family housing management.

It would be difficult to explain residential life and community culture in Korea without discussing multi-family housing. Rather than simply supplying multi-family housing, Korea in 2019 places various efforts across a diverse range of fields into managing the supplied multi-family housing and further creating a new residential community culture. We hope that readers around the world will garner an understanding of multi-family housing in Korea, multi-family housing management systems and Korean's living and community culture, and utilize this book as a useful material in developing housing policies.

President of the Korea Research Institute of Housing Management
Seong-Kyu Ha

Contents

CHAPTER 1

Background behind Development of Multi-Family Housing in Korea

CHAPTER 1

Background behind Development of Multi-Family Housing in Korea

Seong-Kyu Ha,
President of the Korea Research Institute of Housing Management

1. Concept of multi-family housing

W. F. Smith (1971) established the multi-faceted conceptual definition of housing as a shelter in a fixed location required by human beings to lead an internal and personal family life, and a haven and dwelling for the carrying out of daily basic functions of human beings, encompassing aspects such as privacy, geographical location and investment. The definition of housing emphasizes its socioeconomic implications as well as the understanding of its physical characteristics.

Housing is conceptualized in a multi-dimensional manner as "physical facilities, economic commodities with the nature of durable goods and investment goods, social goods or collective goods as a basic unit of social organizations, a summation of various services, and a part of the national economy as a political means to produce wealth (Ha, 2010)."

Housing simultaneously possesses use value and exchange value of its residents. Use value-centered housing includes non-profit welfare housing (public rental housing), and exchange value-centered housing refers to those intended for sale or transaction purposes within the market mechanism. Notably, as housing in the modern society exists as an object of wealth accumulation and possession, it connotes the multi-faceted concepts of not only living facilities representing social status and income, but also valuable investment properties.

The legal and administrative classifications of housing are not uniformly consistent across the Housing Act, the Enforcement Decree of the Building Act, and Statistics Korea's Population and Housing Census.

The Housing Act classifies housing into detached housing, multi-family housing, national housing and urban residential housing. The term "housing" means all or a portion of a building structured so that members of a household can reside independently from other households for a long term and the land attached thereto, and is classified into detached housing and multi-family housing. The term "detached housing" means housing structured so that one household can reside independently from other households within one building, and the term "multi-family housing" means housing structured so that each household that uses all or some of walls, hallways, stairs or other facilities of a building can reside independently from other households within one building, and the kinds and scope thereof shall be prescribed by Presidential Decree.

Appendix 1 of the Enforcement Decree of the Building Act classifies detached houses into detached houses, multi-user houses, multi-unit houses(Dagagu)[1] and official residences.[2] The Enforcement Decree of the Building Act defines multi-family housing as housing structured so that each household that uses all or some of walls, hallways, stairs or other facilities of a building can reside independently from other households within one building, and divides them into apartment houses, tenement houses, multi-household houses(Dasedae)[3] and dormitories, depending on

1 Dagagu housing is a type of detached house where several households can reside in the house. The entire house except the basement level shall be three stories or less, and the total area of floor area shall be less than 660 square meters (200 pyeong). Dagagu houses cannot be sold individually because they cannot be registered separately.

2 Appendix 1 of the Enforcement Decree of the Building Act

3 Dasedae housing refers to a house with a floor area of less than 660 square meters

the number of floors and total floor area.[4]

The Population and Housing Census divides housing into detached houses, apartments, row houses, Dasedae housing, and houses within commercial buildings, and reclassifies detached houses into general detached houses and multi-household detached houses. As shown above, the classification of housing types varies depending on regulations and research purposes.

Historical forms of multi-family housing and collective social living can be found in the Roman Empire. The world's first apartment can be traced back to an "insula" rented to ordinary people during ancient Rome, about 2,000 years ago. These five- to six-story insulae are considered to have been the equivalent of modern multi-purpose buildings. The ground-level floor of insulae was used for shops, with living spaces placed upstairs. The upper classes and the wealthy in ancient Rome lived in a domus, a detached house that was generally grander in scale, and constructed insulae to collect high rent. Since the initial insulae were built using timber and prone to fire and collapse, Emperor Augustus (r. 27 B.C. to 14 A.D.) established laws stipulating a height limit for buildings up to 20 meters and the use of bricks in building the lower part of insulae (Korean Dictionary Research Publishing, 2004).

The modern concept of apartments emerged with the advent of the Industrial Revolution in Britain in the 18th century. The Enclosure Movement forced farmers off of their land and to migrate to cities, resulting in the overpopulation of urban areas and a shortage of housing. As the Enclosure Movement compelled farmers to relocate to towns and cities, the resulting abundant pool of low-income workers had an impact on urban industrial production and the Industrial Revolution. Apartments

and a floor area of less than four stories. Dasedae houses can be registered by households because they are built to accommodate multiple households within a building. They are also characterized by a single unit of sale or ownership. (Annex 1 to the Enforcement Decree of the Building Act)

4 Article 2(2) of the Enforcement Decree of the Housing Act and Appendix 1 of the Enforcement Decree of the Building Act

were introduced as a suitable type of housing for these low-income workers. To solve housing problems facing the urban poor, the British government supplied collective housing with a better environment by establishing building regulations. This is regarded as the origin of modern apartment housing.

2. Background of apartment supply

The history of apartments in Korea began alongside industrialization and urbanization. Urbanization resulted in higher population density and subsequently housing shortages, which led to the construction of apartments to alleviate the situation. The following examines the background behind apartment supply in each period.

1) Laying the foundation for housing supply during the 1960s and 70s

Korea paved the way for the construction of apartments in the 1960s. Housing policy targets were officially introduced for the first time in the first five-year economic development plan of 1962. However, the Korean government invested a mere 1.7% of the gross national product (GNP) in the housing industry between 1962 and 1967. During the period of the second five-year economic development plan, which commenced in 1967, the government accelerated its effort to expand the housing supply through public sector entities such as the Korea National Housing Corporation (KNHC) and the Seoul Special City.

The government founded the Korea Housing Bank, later renamed as the Housing and Commercial Bank, in 1967, and implemented financial support policies. During this period, the Chung-Hee Park government actively borrowed from the U.S. and Japan, and the growing demand resulting from the Vietnam War contributed to an increase in exports. Consequently, the Korean economy recorded explosive growth with an annual average growth rate of 8.8% between 1962 and 1971. With the beginning of social overhead capital (SOC) projects including the construction of roads and harbors, the construction industry grew by 17.4% on average each year during the period of the first five-year economic development plan, and the country's manufacturing capacity for cement also increased. In addition, the advancement of industrialization encouraged people to migrate to cities, driving up the demand for housing.

The public sector played a significant role in supplying housing in the 1970s. Despite the growing need for housing supply centered around major cities, a lack of construction companies with reliable business capabilities made it difficult to leave housing supply in the hands of the private sector. The Korea Housing Administration was renamed as the Korea National Housing Corporation (KNHC) with the enactment of the Korea National Housing Corporation Act in 1962 and played a central role in building apartments. The KNHC constructed large-scale housing complexes such as the country's first apartment complex Mapo Apartment (1962), Hangang Mansion (1970 to 1971) and Banpo Jugong Apartment Complex 1 (1971 to 1974). In particular, the KNHC introduced today's housing presale system by utilizing model houses for the first time in the country.

On top of this, the Seoul Special City served as a mainstay in the housing supply alongside the KNHC. The capital city conducted a plan to build 2,000 citizen apartment buildings encompassing a total of 90,000 households for three years from 1969 to 1971. Despite its brief suspension due to the breakdown of Wawoo Apartment in 1970, the city's plan was completed by supplying 16,963 households in 426 apartment buildings across 32 districts of Seoul.

Inflation caused land and housing prices to skyrocket in the late 1970s. Meanwhile, the speculative demand for apartments soared as well. Starting with Mokhwa Apartment in Yeouido, Seoul, which was sold in March 1977 at a subscription competition rate of 45:1, Hwagok Apartment, sold in March of the same year, recorded a subscription competition rate of 178:1, indicating the overheated competition for apartment subscription. Moreover, the government devised a variety of policies to promote housing and urban development, which encouraged more private construction companies to participate in apartment construction after the mid-1970s. As a result, a total of 300,107 housing units were built in 1978, which included 99,727 apartment households.

The Park government established a national plan to build 2,500,000 houses over a decade and set the criteria to funnel public funds into the construction of 1,108,500 households. Moreover, the government established the Housing Construction Promotion Act in 1972 and institutionalized its financial support for private sector housing development projects. The policy took shape as an extensive urban development plan for Seoul districts south of the Han River, collectively known as the Gangnam area, so that the Gangnam area encompassing Jamsil, Banpo and Apgujeong became designated as apartment districts, attracting private sector builders into the construction of large-scale apartment complexes.

The government overhauled the Housing Construction Promotion Act in 1977. Accordingly, the registration system for housing construction companies and the designation system for excellent builders were newly established, and the KNHC and designated construction companies were given the right to issue redeemable housing bonds, which laid the groundwork for the growth of private construction companies. These policies encouraged large companies, which grew with the help of SOC projects and the Middle East construction boom, into actively conducting domestic housing projects, thereby contributing to a rapid growth in the domestic housing construction industry. Meanwhile, during this period, the subscription system and the regulation of sales prices were established as part of policies designed to prevent apartment speculation (Lim, 2005).

2) Boom and depression during the 1980s and 90s

In the early 1980s, Korea suffered an economic crisis due to the second oil shock and the global economic crisis in 1979. The new military junta instituted economic stability policies by scaling down investment in the heavy chemical industry and closing down insolvent companies. Under the economic circumstances, the housing construction market went into a slump. The annual housing supply sharply fell from 300,107 households in 1978 to 252,048 households in 1979, 211,537 households in 1980 and 149,847 households in 1981. The annual number of houses supplied hovered just above 200,000 households until 1985. The economic crisis of the early 1980s turned into an opportunity in the late 1980s, however, as the extreme lack of housing supply served as a driving force behind a boom in the housing market over the period between the late 1980 and the 1990s.

Korea and other emerging industrialized countries in Asia benefited the most from the so-called "three lows" such as lows in the U.S. dollar, interest rates and oil prices in the mid-1980s. The Korean economy continued its trend of growth from 1986, and reached its peak in 1988 with the opening of the Seoul Olympics. From 1988 to 1990, Korea even posted a large trade surplus. The economic recovery and the trade surplus increased liquidity, leading to another boom in the real estate market starting in 1988.

With its inauguration in 1988, the Tae-Woo Roh government announced a national plan to construct 2,000,000 households by 1992 with an aim to stabilize housing prices and reached this goal ahead of schedule in 1991 thanks to the buoyancy of the real estate market. The Roh government's efforts to expand the supply of housing sites, such as the national plan to build 2,000,000 households and the development of five New Towns around the capital area to supply 300,000 households, resulted in a surge in housing supply.

The housing site development initiative was designed for the first five New Towns and expanded to include Goyang (Gyeonggi), Suji (Yongin), Yeongtong (Suwon) and Haeundae (Busan). In the past, the KNHC and other public sector entities were instrumental in supplying multi-family housing, while private sector construction companies came to occupy the majority in this period. With the expansion of the housing supply and the housing market, the housing construction capability of private builders greatly improved. The KNHC's share in the annual apartment construction hovered around 30% until 1985, but the figure fell to around 15% after 1989. Notably, large construction companies built 69,322 households in 1989, exceeding the housing supply by the KNHC with 50,682 households. The private sector supply increased to 213,990 households in 1995, almost three times greater than that of the KNHC with 70,292 households. As shown above, the market competition between many private construction companies heightened the keenness for product development and marketing.

3) Expansion and reduction in apartment supply in the 2000s

In the 1990s, the housing penetration rate exceeded 86% due to the development of the first New Towns. A decrease in the demand for housing purchases sustained the stagnation of the housing market. Although apartment construction companies such as Dong Ah Construction, Woosung Construction and Woobang Corporation took the lead in the housing construction industry in the 1980s and 90s, they fell into bankruptcy in succession due to financial difficulties stemming from the rising number of unsold apartments.

The housing industry enjoyed a boom again following the crisis. The 1998 IMF financial crisis sharply diminished housing sales. Housing price and supply jumped owing to the shortage of housing supply in the early 2000s. After 2001, apartment prices began to suddenly rise in the capital area and the apartment market was so brisk that there was a saying that apartment prices in Gangnam and New Towns such as Bundang rose higher every morning.

After the emergence of Korea's first multipurpose residential buildings in 2002 with Dogok-dong's Tower Palace, the myth of "Gangnam never fails" essentially became an established fact. Tower Palace heralded the golden age of upscale multipurpose residential buildings such as I'Park in Samseong-dong, Hyperion in Mok-dong and Park View in Bundang.[5]

The craze for apartments started in the Gangnam area and spread to the entire capital through the New Town Project. During his campaign, then Seoul mayor Myung-Bak Lee pledged to develop the Gangbuk area, the Seoul districts north of the Han River, by conducting the New Town Project. Eunpyeong, Gireum and Wangsimni were designated as pilot districts. The craze for apartment development peaked with Pangyo New Town: In 2005, 16,157 households in 31 apartment complexes were sold simultaneously, and the sale of Pungseong Sinmiju Apartment posted a remarkable competition rate of up to 2,073:1 in May 2006.

To address the sudden rise in apartment prices revolving around the Gangnam area, the Moo-Hyun Roh government devised restrictions on loan-to-value (LTV) and debt-to-income (DTI) ratios, and introduced the gross real estate tax. Despite such strong price regulations, the government failed to prevent housing price from rising. The price of Eunma Apartment in Gangnam-gu, based on the sale area of 35 *pyeong*, skyrocketed from 70 million won in 1988 to 225 million won in 2001 and to 1.13 billion won in 2007. The sharp rise in real estate prices in the mid-2000s was attributable to the fact that the Participatory Government paid compensation expenses valued at about 98.57 trillion won over five years in a bid to establish business cities and innovative cities across the country, with 90% of the expenses paid in cash, which led liquid funds in the market to flow into the real estate market.

Apartment prices continued to rise across the entire capital area until 2007, and the upward trend slowed down in September 2008 because of the global financial crisis. The apartment market has since remained sluggish to date. Overall, the apartment market in Korea has repeated the pattern of "recovery after stagnation" for the past five decades.

5 In general, redevelopment and apartment reconstruction projects in the 2000s presented plans to build 30- to 40-story apartment buildings. In July 2009, the Enforcement Decree of the Building Act stipulated that the term "skyscraper" is defined as a building at least 50 floors or 200 meters tall.

Figure 1 'Recovery after stagnation' of apartment market in Korea

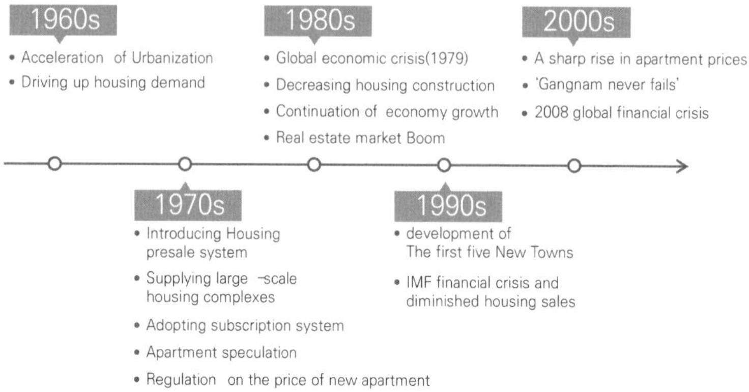

3. Apartments: A symbol of economic growth and desire

French geographer Valérie Gelézeau called Korea the "republic of apartments," which is also the title of her book, *The Republic of Apartments*, that was written after her visit to Korea. Aside from their primary function as housing, urban apartments are considered as a symbol of "modernization" and "living revolution." Apartments ranging from the country's first apartment Mapo Apartment of Seoul in 1961 to the 60-story Tower Palace in 2002, which opened a new era of multipurpose residential buildings, transformed the residential life of Seoul citizens and the skyline of the capital.

The high-rise trend boosted the construction of tower-type apartments, in which households of an apartment building are built to face three or four sides instead of facing the same direction.

The reason why Seoul and other cities in Korea saw a growing number of high-rise apartments does not lie in the country's limited land space, but rather in the Korea-specific "construction economy" under the aim to raise excess profits and land prices by driving up the floor area ratio by around 300% to 500%.

(Figure 2) Tower-type apartment

Source: The Korea Apartment News (2018.10.10)

A number of significant changes also took place in relation to apartment structures since the 1970s. The most notable was central heating. Hangang Mansion in Dongbu Ichon-dong (1970) introduced a central heating system and installed radiator heaters around the whole house, instead of using the traditional Korean floor heating system of *ondol*, for the first time in the country. Banpo Jugong Apartment Complex 1 (1971) adopted the *ondol* system only for the master room and used radiators for other rooms including the living room. The most significant change to apartment construction during the period was the distribution of "flat-type" apartments, or so-called "matchbox" apartments.

(Figure 3) Flat-type apartment

Source: The Korea Apartment News (2015.04.22)

Large-scale corporations in Korea increasingly grew in size by generating enormous income through apartment construction. Valérie Gelézeau, author of *The Republic of Apartments*, pointed out that Western apartment construction was planned as national housing, mainly for workers, while Korean apartments represent a "condensed symbol" of the Korean development model, which was devised by the country's authoritarian governments in partnership with conglomerates, or *chaebol*.

Apartments may originate from Europe, but they have evolved in a very unique way in Korea. At present, apartments accommodate over half of the population. They contain symbolic meanings embodying the development and economic growth of Korean cities; on the other hand, they attract criticism as a means of moneymaking and an object of speculative desire.

The invention of reinforced concrete structures and elevators in the mid-19th century allowed high-rise buildings to be built, and many cities around the world continue to construct super high-rise buildings in competition. Historically, French architect Le Corbusier (1887-1965) deserves special mention with regard to high-rise apartments. Le Corbusier theorized that the construction of taller buildings may allow more civic and green spaces to be secured for residents, resulting in improved quality of life.

Today, high-rise buildings continue to be built in Korea. Seoul's Lotte World Tower, standing 123 stories and 555 meters high, became the sixth tallest skyscraper in the world and the tallest in the country. Out of 123 stories, floors 42 to 71 are reserved for upscale residences accommodating more than 200 households. In the mid-1980s, residential skyscrapers of 20 stories or higher began to be constructed, and super high-rise apartments continue to occupy Seoul and the metropolitan area.

There are extremely mixed views on the construction of skyscrapers for residential purpose. Firstly, advocates for super high-rise apartment buildings regard the construction of residential skyscrapers as the optimal strategy to create pleasant and convenient spaces in densely-populated large cities. In other words, the maximization of urban land use will enhance economic efficiency. As architect Le Corbusier remarked, the construction of higher buildings enables urban residents to enjoy parks and social service facilities, which will improve their quality of living. From the business aspect, the higher apartment buildings go, the higher their prices are set. Therefore, the rising demand for skyscrapers guarantees higher liquidity.

On the other hand, residence in super high-rise apartments entails many difficulties. Among them, to name a few, are frequent traffic congestions around residential skyscraper complexes in the country's large cities, along with safety-related anxiety including large-scale fires. Many research findings indicate that high-rise apartments negatively impact their residents' health. According to reports, residents of high-rise apartments are more than twice as likely to visit healthcare clinics as those who live in five-story-or-lower apartments. Another problem is that the management expenses of high-rise apartments are three to four times more expensive than those of ordinary apartments. It remains to be seen whether high-rise apartments will continue to maintain their position as the preferred type of housing in the future in comparison to low-rise ones.

References

Park, C. S. (2006). *The Cultural History of Apartments.* Paju: Sallim Books.

Gelézeau, V. (2007). *The Republic of Apartments.* (Hye-Yeon Gil, Trans.). Seoul: Humanitas.

Lim, S. H. (2005). *A Half Century of Housing Policies.* Seoul: Kimoondang.

Ha, S. K. (2010). *Housing Policy and Practice in Korea.* Seoul: Parkyoungsa.

Ha, S. K. (2018). *The Housing Question in Korea.* Seoul: Parkyoungsa.

The Compilation Committee of the Korean Dictionary Research Publishing. (2004). *Encyclopedia of Arts (Terminology).* Korean Dictionary Research Publishing.

Smith, W. F. (1971). *Housing: The Social and Economic Elements.* Berkeley: University of California Press.

CHAPTER 2

Significance of Multi-Family Housing Management

CHAPTER 2

Significance of Multi-Family Housing Management

Seong-Kyu Ha,
President of the Korea Research Institute of Housing Management

1. Functions of multi-family housing

Apartments are spaces in which privacy is secured as one of the most important features of housing. In other words, apartments refer to a private space with access to public spaces or shared spaces at the same time. Once residents leave their apartments, the outside space does not consist of private spaces but rather shared spaces such as hallways, parks, stairs, elevators and children's playgrounds. Accordingly, apartments possess a variety of functions(Ha, 2014).

Figure 1 Functions of multi-family housing

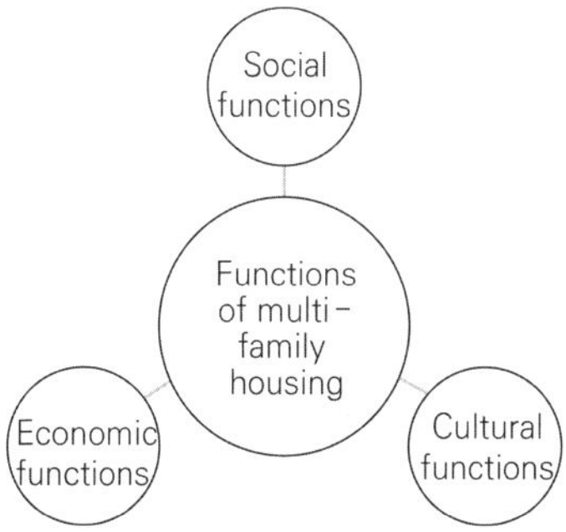

1) Social functions of multi-family housing

First, apartments offer community functions. Those who reside in apartments have to coexist with other residents, namely neighbors, within an apartment complex. Apartment residents encounter their neighbors in hallways and elevators every day. They are obliged to live closer to their neighbors in a spatial sense compared to those living in detached housing. Frequent contact with neighbors is inevitable for apartment residents, since there are many shared spaces. In this sense, apartment houses involve community elements in the spatial sense. However, multi-family housing complexes can be prone to conflicts arising from problems such as between-floor noise and parking issues.

Second, the social functions of apartments are related to "social capital," which can be defined as trust, norms and networks based on the characteristics of the social structure (Bourdieu, 1986; Coleman, 1988; Putnam, 2004; Fukuyama, 1995).

Social capital is distinguished from other types of capitals in two aspects: First, the creation and activation of social capital require at least two people; and second, social capital is an accumulated stock into which the result of its utilization flows (Grootaert & van Bastelaer, 2002). Therefore, residential community-based social capital is established by the social relations among residents within the set spatial scope of a community and reinforced through the accumulation of reciprocity and trust among them.

The network and trust built between neighbors provide individuals with a sense of safety and belonging. For example, if an individual's neighbors cannot be trusted and constantly cause caution and anxiety, it will result in significant negative impacts both mentally and physically, and further serve as severe detriments to everyday life. If residents can trust their neighbors and create a human network based on mutual faith, however, this would positively influence the quality of life and wellbeing of the individuals and their family.

Moreover, in cases where residents function as resources by expanding opportunities for joint participation, simultaneously sharing value and exchanging useful information and data within the residential community, social capital can be defined as resources shared by members of the community. The concepts of individual and shared resources can apply not only to residential community but also the workplace and other official and unofficial organizations.

The sharing of concerns and interests and the formation of social consensus among members of a community may significantly support and positively impact all of the members (Arefi, 2003). However, social capital has limitations in that it provides no direct benefits for those outside the community concerned and is exclusively enjoyed among members of the organization or community. Other limitations include restrictions of individual freedom and possible concerns over the weakening of norms (Portes, 1988). Importantly, it is necessary to differentiate between bonding and bridging social capital. Bonding social capital builds on closed relations with family members, neighbors, friends and coworkers, while bridging social capital is based on weak ties between those who do not share a common ground.

2) Economic functions of multi-family housing

Housing is a durable good that accounts for the most important and the biggest asset of a household's total income among the low-income bracket in Korea. Housing costs occupy over 20% of household expenditure for the majority of Koreans. The Schwabe index refers to a measure of housing costs relative to household expenses. Although higher income generally leads to higher housing costs, for rent in particular, the proportion of money spent on housing out of the total household expenses actually decreases. This principle is called Schwabe's law after the German statistician Heinrich Schwabe. The Schwabe index is used as an indicator to measure household expenditure, along with the Engel coefficient. According to Schwabe's law, the high proportion of housing costs relative to household expenses in the low-income bracket exacerbates housing instability.

The Hyundai Research Institute published a research report titled "Full-time Homemakers Aged 40s and 50s Lead Consumption" in September 2013. The research findings indicated that the highest proportion of respondents (22.1%) answered that housing-related outlays including monthly rent and/or long-term deposits on leased homes (*jeonse*) and management expenses posed the biggest financial burden, followed by food costs (21.5%) and educational spending (21.4%). By income bracket, the burden of housing and food costs was greater in proportion among lower income brackets. Those with higher income were found to pay more for children's education.[1] As housing costs constitute essential living costs, they cannot be scaled down easily. Stagnation or decrease in actual income inevitably forces an increase in the proportion of housing costs relative to total spending. According to the Hyundai Research Institute, the Schwabe index, which refers to the proportion of total household expenditure spent on housing, continued to increase from 9.71% in 2007 and reached 10.15% in 2011, the highest figure since records began. Apartments are a common type of housing for ordinary households in urban cities, who dream of possessing their own house by purchasing an apartment unit.

3) Cultural functions of multi-family housing

Multi-family housing management prioritizes maintaining the maximum value of multi-family housing by allowing it to serve its housing functions to the maximum extent until the end of its lifespan and eventually extending its lifespan to preserve its value to the maximum extent. A key aspect of housing management is conducting all activities aimed to

1 This survey was conducted from September 14 to 20, 2013 through telephone interview s with adult men and women aged 20 or older across the country. The sampling is based on the minimum allocation by region and the population ratio. The stated confidence level was 95% with a margin of error of +/− 3.08 percentage points. (See http://www.newsis.com/ar_detail/view.html?ar_id=NISX20130904_0012333602&cID=10401&pID=10400. December 14, 2013)

increase economic, cultural and environmental values of residence by managing multi-family housing, related facilities and surrounding environments.

Forms of housing vary in different periods, areas and social systems, and the size and type of housing have served as a determinant of the owner's social status or class. Social changes introduce new types of housing, creating a new living culture. As long as people voluntarily participate in this process and live in houses that aptly accommodate their lives, the future remains bright and forthcoming generations will also lead beautiful lives amidst this process.

When it comes to multi-family housing management, the characteristics and significance of residential culture are vital from the perspective of the "community." The location of housing determines its residential culture, which means that a residential culture is established and developed based on endemism, norms, customs and preferences.

With regard to multi-family housing, Koreans are less interested in identifying external spaces or points of contact when viewing apartment showrooms. They solely focus on exclusive residential area (unit plan), interior materials, floor plan and room size. The perceived scope of living space in daily life was reduced to the unit plan and influenced by the presale system and efforts to strengthen marketing activities. To reiterate, a one-sided residential culture is taking root, whereby residents fail to incorporate public spaces for interactions among residents into their own living space.

Furthermore, apartments serve as a reflection of social class. For example, living in apartments located in Gangnam or Gangbuk demonstrates the gap among income brackets or socioeconomic class as well as the separation of housing class. In Korea, the size or area of apartments sometimes represents the economic level of a household. This Korea-specific apartment culture is taking shape as a yardstick to determine social class formation and socioeconomic level.

With regard to apartment complex management, the properties of residential culture cannot be disregarded. For example, apartment complexes inhabited by a large number of elderly residents require efforts to encourage and develop cultural facilities and activities that are best suited for elderly residents. Public rental apartments with a dense population of low-income residents must take into account occupants' socioeconomic perspectives in establishing the residential culture. "Residence" connotes characteristics that are inseparable from cultural properties. The management of apartment complexes in the future will require efforts to closely research and analyze such cultural elements and maintain positive and progressive cultural properties.

2. Significance of multi-family housing management

Housing management and its significance can be largely defined from three perspectives. First, housing is an object to be managed as a physical object. Multi-family housing encompasses the entire physical living space including apartment buildings and auxiliary buildings. Housing is both an important asset of individual households and a home to sustain the family. Housing management stems from the need to maintain and manage houses to remain as pleasant and safe as possible and to simultaneously retain or increase property value (exchange value for the owner).

Second, housing management includes the lives of those who use the physical facilities entailed by housing, namely their occupants. Multi-family housing management is not limited to the maintenance of apartment buildings as physical facilities, but they should be managed in a way that improves the safety, pleasantness, network and quality of life of their residents.

Third, as housing management is related to not only physical facilities but also occupants who reside in them, apartment complexes or communities must also be taken into account. When housing management fails to guarantee the maintenance of safe and livable communities or estates, the individual houses within them cannot be expected to serve as a home and provide an adequate quality of life.

Housing cannot be used infinitely, but rather ages over time. A core value of housing management lies in efforts to minimize and preclude a wide range of inconveniences, threats to safety and loss of property (decrease in value) caused by deterioration. In this sense, housing management should follow the principles below (Ha, 2014; Bang, 2013).

1) Provide high-quality services

Housing management should guarantee services to ensure the safety of occupants and minimize inconveniences. In principle, housing management should offer all of the services that allow owners and occupants to live safely and lead a pleasant and comfortable residential life without inconveniences.

2) Maintain the asset value of housing

Housing comprises important assets of individual households with exchange and user value. Therefore, housing should be managed to allow the maximization of these two values. A significant purpose of housing management is to preserve property value for occupants and owners.

3) Expand social capital

The social environment surrounding housing is critical. Housing should be managed in a way to vitalize the social atmosphere, networks and communal activities of apartment complexes and communities, and create positive and progressive social environments. Interactions among residents should be promoted to minimize or prevent conflicts among them, and social capital (trust, norms and networks) should be boosted through housing management.

4) Promote eco-friendliness and sustainable development

Housing connotes the spatial scope of a city or area and is included in the entire environment. The health and safety of residents may be influenced by the districts in which their houses are located or the natural and artificial environments of the entire area. Therefore, multi-family housing places an emphasis on greenery and parks, energy use, pleasantness of shared spaces, and the ecological environment within apartment complexes. There is a need for eco-friendly and green housing management to meet the global goals of the United Nations and other international organizations with regard to prevention of global warming, in addition to implementing green cities, ecological cities and sustainable development.[2]

5) Maintain characteristics of public goods

Housing management, particularly multi-family housing management, involves a wide range of issues. Among them, the foremost to be considered is related to the characteristic of multi-family housing as public goods. For example, the security, safety, cleaning, maintenance of common facilities (equipment) and other management services required in multi-family housing complexes are used by and exert an influence on individuals, although they are uniformly provided to all occupants. The services belonging to all the people living in multi-family housing complexes have elements of public goods such as non-competitiveness and non-excludability.

Non-competitiveness means that no matter how many people participate in the consumption of goods and services, their availability to each individual remains intact. Fresh air or picturesque views in public parks do not require additional costs whether they are consumed by one person or

2 Sustainable development (SD) is a series of ways to preserve the environment, eradicate poverty and create economic growth in a way that does not destroy natural resources in the short run for the purpose of long-term growth. SD is defined as development that fulfills the needs of the current generation to an extent that does not compromise the possibilities for the next generations to satisfy their own needs. The concept of SD is traced back to the 1987 UN report "Our Common Future" by Gro Harlem Brundtland (Ha et al., *How to Make Cities Sustainable*, Boseonggak, 2008).

ten people. Non-excludability means that there is no way to prevent the consumption of goods and services by those who wish to consume them without paying costs. When a person plants trees and they produce fresh air, he/she cannot restrict other people from inhaling the air exuded by the trees. Noncompetitive and nonexclusive goods are sometimes inadequately supplied by the market. Such goods are needed by the entire society.

3. Urgent issues of multi-family housing

On December 15, 2013, a fire tore through an apartment in Hwamyeong-dong, Buk-gu, Busan Metropolitan City, killing Ms. Hong and her three children. The mother was found on a balcony, hugging her two children tightly in her arms. The police announced that she had contacted emergency services for the fire, which had started at the entrance, and escaped to the balcony with her children, only to succumb to toxic gases. The fact that these lives were lost despite the normal operation of the fire protection system including autonomous fire detection facilities and emergency alarms shows that there are fundamental problems with the safety systems of living spaces (*Joongang Ilbo*, December 16, 2013).

The news article reminds readers of the significance of multi-family housing management, especially safety management and educational training. Accidents occurring in multi-family housing are frequently attributable to not only natural disasters but also mismanagement and user negligence. Such accidents occur in various settings such as elevators and children's playgrounds. Conflicts among neighbors over criminal activities, between-floor noise and parking-related problems are on the rise and have long since emerged as social issues.

Figure 2 Examples of apartment accidents

Source: The Korea Apartment News (2017.10.18; 2019.06.12)

According to recent press reports, apartment management companies, housing managers and occupants' representatives are often involved in illicit acts and corruption in general. More specifically, special crackdowns conducted by the National Policy Agency from March to May in 1999 uncovered cases of illicit acts in 1,996 (22.5%) of 8,864 apartment complexes around the country and announced that the amount of damage caused by embezzlement and breach of duty reached around 17.08 billion won. Occupants' representatives received kickbacks from insurance companies in exchange for purchasing fire insurance as well as contracting maintenance work, and officials in women's associations of apartment communities demanded that vendors pay fees to do business within the apartment complexes or to sponsor various events, all of which were considered common practices (*Chosun Ilbo*, May 6, 2013).

Imminent issues regarding multi-family housing management can be summarized as follows. First, multi-family housing management has shifted its focus from the supplier to the consumer. This demonstrates a significant departure from the past, when there were no issues in selling new apartments. Since the asset value of apartments has long been on the increase due to the gap created by short supply and excessive demand, the focus on multi-family housing management has decreased in comparison.

Second, multi-family housing management has also shifted its focus from hardware to software, or from physical to socioeconomic aspects. Although problems with poor construction and defects still remain, issues related to apartment management such as corruption, illicit acts, contract methods and lack of ethics are considered to be even more grave. In the past, Korea's housing management system had concentrated on hardware concerning maintenance, safety and facilities as per the Housing Act, the Special Act on the Safety Control and Maintenance of Establishments, and Acts on firefighting, water supply, electricity and gas facilities.

Third, apartments and apartment complexes are perceived as not only physical living spaces but also investment goods, and the management scope is expanding from facilities management to asset management. From this perspective, multi-family housing management places greater emphasis on the living environment and socioeconomic stability rather than on physical stability. Characteristics of residents in multi-family housing are changing and becoming more differentiated both demographically and sociologically. To name a few, the number of one-person households, elderly housing and multicultural households is increasing. There are growing and diversifying needs for socioeconomic services as well as the existing maintenance services of physical facilities.

Fourth, one of the imminent problems facing multi-family housing management is the conflicting or symbiotic relationship between decision-making bodies and execution bodies. The relationship between the council of occupants' representatives (decision-making body) and the management entity (execution body) should be considered to be horizontal, not vertical. The management entity is frequently replaced upon the request of occupants' representatives on account of a lack of objective work evaluation criteria.

Fifth, inadequate job security for housing managers continues to be an issue. This is a systematic problem resulting from the fact that the number of housing managers far outstrips social demand. Moreover, the dismissal of housing managers tends to rely on the interests of the council of occupants' representatives due to the inadequate criteria for their dismissal and the lack of objective evaluation criteria for their work. An institutional framework is needed to evaluate the work performance of housing managers in an objective way(Ha, 2018).

References

Bang, K. S. (2013). *Theory of Multi-Family Housing Management.* Seoul: Buyonsa.

Ha, S. K. et al. (2014). *Contemporary Multi−family Housing Management: Theory and Practice,* Seoul: Parkyoungsa.

Ha, S. K. et al. (2018). *A New Paradigm for Multifamily Housing Management.* Seoul: Parkyoungsa.

Ha, S. K. et al. (2008). *How to Make Cities Sustainable.* Seoul: Boseonggak.

Arefi, M. (2003). Revisiting the Los Angeles Neighborhood Initiative (LANI): Lessons for Planners. *Journal of planning education and research,* 22(4), 384.

Bourdieu, P. (1986). The Forms of Capital, in J. G. Richardson (Ed.) *The Handbook of Theory and Research for the Sociology of Education,* pp.241-258, New York: Greenwood Press.

Coleman, J. (1998). *Foundations of Social Theory.* Cambridge: Belknap Press of Harvard University Press.

Edwards, B., & Foley, M. W. (1998). Civil Society and Social Capital Beyond Putnam. *American Behavioral Scientist,* 42(1), 124-139.

Fukuyama, F. (2004). *State-Building: Governance and World Order in the 21st Century.* Cornell University Press.

Granovetter, M. (1973). The Strength of Weak Ties. *American Journal of Sociology,* 78, 1360-1380.

Grootaert, C., & van Bastelaer, T. (2002). *Understanding and Measuring Social Capital: A Multi-Disciplinary Tool for Practitioners.* Washington, DC: World Bank.

Putnam, R. D. (2004). *Democracies in Flux: The Evolution of Social Capital in Contemporary Society.* Oxford: Oxford University Press.

Portes, A. (1998). Social Capital: Its Origins and Applications in Modern Sociology. *Annual Review of Sociology,* 24(1), 1-24.

CHAPTER 3

Multi-Family Housing Management System

CHAPTER 3

Multi-Family Housing Management System

Kwan-Ho Myong,
Legal Affairs Officer of the Korea Housing Managers Association

1. About the multi-family housing management system

In Korea, the Multi-Family Housing Management Act has been enacted and entered into effect as the law that prescribes matters on the management of multi-family housing. In this chapter, the Act will serve as basic reference to discuss Korea's multi-family housing management system. As the purpose of the Act is the "transparent, safe, and efficient management of multi-family housing," details of the multi-family housing management system were also established for the same purpose.

2. History of laws on multi-family housing management

1) Enactment and enforcement of the Multi-Family Housing Management Act

The Multi-Family Housing Management Act, which prescribes matters on the management of multi-family housing, was enacted in August 2015 and entered into effect in August 2016. Prior to the enactment and enforcement of the Act, provisions on the "management" of multi-family housing were included in legislation on the "supply and construction" of multi-family housing. As such, not many years have passed since matters on the management of multi-family housing were codified into a dedicated law and entered into effect.

2) Laws on the management of multi-family housing before the enactment of the Multi-Family Housing Management Act

The first law on the management of multi-family housing in Korea, prior to the Multi-Family Housing Management Act, was the Public Housing Act enacted in 1963. However, the purpose of the Act was to set forth articles under which the Korea National Housing Corporation and local governments could jointly construct public housing with the support of the government and supply it to non-homeowners. Therefore, the Public Housing Act mainly stipulated matters on the construction of public housing, while leaving the details on housing management to be defined autonomously by each business entity or only stipulating the eligibility for occupants of public housing.

Subsequently, the Housing Construction Promotion Act was established in 1972, which still mainly dealt with matters concerning the "supply of housing and relevant financing and fund management." However, the Act was amended significantly in 1977 (December 31, 1977) to stipulate provisions on entrusted management by housing management service providers, as well as autonomous management by occupants, and adding a provision that a certificate of qualification as a housing manager was required for individuals to work as a qualified housing manager. In 1978, the Act was partially amended, and related lower-level ordinances such as the Decree on Multi-Family Housing Management and the Rules of Multi-Family Housing Management were established as a Presidential Decree and a Ministerial Decree, respectively. Most of the institutions and practices specified in the current Multi-Family Housing Management Act originated from the aforementioned laws.

With regard to multi-family housing management, the amended Housing

Construction Promotion Act stipulated the following: 1. in cases where multi-family housing and its auxiliary facilities are used for purposes other than those specified under the project plan, or in cases of expansion or rebuilding, the approval of the Minister of Construction shall be required; 2. housing management may be conducted by the housing manager, instead of autonomous management by the occupant; 3. the business entity's (or the housing construction business entity registered pursuant to applicable laws) obligations in respect to the repairing of defects; 4. the occupant's obligation of paying fees for the replacement and repair of main facilities of multi-family housing (reserves for special repairs) and uses of the fees; and 5. matters on the housing manager's license, management methods, and job details. The Decree on Multi-Family Housing Management was more detailed than the Housing Construction Promotion Act and included regulations for the autonomous organization of occupants (the council of occupants' representatives), provisions on management expenses items and payment methods by household, and amendments to and details of multi-family housing management rules.

In 2003, the Housing Construction Promotion Act was wholly amended and the Act was renamed as the Housing Act, reflecting the importance of conducting efficient "management" of existing housing in addition to "promoting" the "construction and supply" of housing in response to changed economic and social conditions.

3. Key stipulations of the Multi-Family Housing Management Act

1) Application scope

The Multi-Family Housing Management Act, which prescribes matters on the management of multi-family housing, applies only to multi-family housing among condominium buildings, and the scope of "multi-family housing" includes apartment houses, tenement houses, and multi-household houses. The Housing Act categorizes officetels and dormitories under condominium buildings as "quasi-housing," while the Multi-Family Housing Management Act excludes quasi-housing from its application scope. Condominium buildings excluding multi-family housing are subject to the Act on Ownership and Management of Condominium Buildings.

In addition, the Multi-Family Housing Management Act applies to all types of multi-family housing, but some of its provisions are "mandatory" for multi-family housing with a given number of households (150 or more households in the case of Korea) and the sizable multi-family housing is called "multi-family housing subject to compulsory management." The scope of multi-family housing subject to compulsory management is expected to expand through further amendment of the Act.

2) Structure of the Act

The Multi-Family Housing Management Act is composed of 11 chapters.

Chapter 1 stipulates general provisions including the purpose of the Act, definitions, and relationship to other Acts.

Chapter 2 outlines methods of multi-family housing management by dividing them into autonomous management and entrusted management, and sets forth basic matters related to the two methods.

Chapter 3 stipulates procedures to elect representatives (representative of each building) who will represent occupants, etc. (including users) residing in the multi-family housing and to form a council of occupants' representatives, which is an autonomous organization composed of representatives of each building, and also provides rules on the management and use of multi-family housing to serve as rules of autonomy prescribed by occupants, etc.

Chapter 4 prescribes matters on the enforcement of expenses that occupants, etc. pay in relation to the management of the multi-family housing, including management expenses necessary for the maintenance of multi-family housing.

Chapter 5 provides the management entity's obligation of establishing a long-term repair plan for the common areas of multi-family housing and matters on the accumulation of reserves for long-term repairs, which are necessary for the replacement, maintenance and repair of key facilities in the multi-family housing, and also stipulates that, in cases of using multi-family housing and its auxiliary facilities for purposes other than those specified under the applicable project plan or expanding or rebuilding multi-family housing, permission from or notification of the head of the applicable local government shall be required.

Chapter 6 provides regulations on the business entity's warranty liability, putting up of security deposits for repairing defects, procedures for the repair of defects, and the establishment of a defect examination and dispute mediation committee.

Chapter 7 specifies the requirements for registration as a housing management service provider to serve as a management entity that conducts management work when the entrusted management method is the chosen method of multi-family housing management.

Chapter 8 specifies provisions on the establishment and operation of the "Multi-Family Housing Management Dispute Mediation Committee" to mediate disputes arising out of the management of multi-family housing.

Chapter 9 includes provisions on the establishment of an association of housing managers, etc. and its mutual aid programs.

Chapter 10 is composed of supplementary provisions stipulating that the Minister of Land, Infrastructure and Transport may designate an organization to provide support with regard to the management of multi-family housing, and includes provisions on the establishment and operation of the multi-family housing management information system, local governments' authority to oversee the management of multi-family housing, and Complaint Center of Irregularities in Management of Multi-Family Housing.

Chapter 11 specifies provisions on penalties and administrative fines to be imposed for breaches of any of the applicable provisions.

Hereinafter, a number of key matters will be examined rather than elaborating all of the above-stated provisions. However, matters concerning 1) the housing manager system and 2) management expenses for multi-family housing and reserves for long-term repairs under the long-term repair plan will be discussed in other chapters.

3) Management methods

The Multi-Family Housing Management Act divides the methods for managing multi-family housing into autonomous management and entrusted management. With the former method, occupants residing in multi-family housing directly conduct management work, while in the entrusted management system, management work is entrusted to a housing management service provider.

Once occupants, etc. decide to adopt the autonomous management system, the council of occupants' representatives will form a management body of multi-family housing. Then, the council of occupants' representatives will appoint the head of the management office to serve as the representative of the management body of multi-family housing, and mobilize the technical personnel and equipment necessary for the management of the multi-family housing. Technical personnel refer to persons legally qualified with regard to elevators, electricity, gas, firefighting facilities, etc., suitable for the types and sizes of facilities in the multi-family housing.

If occupants, etc. decide to outsource the management work, the council of occupants' representatives will select a housing management service provider and conclude an entrustment agreement. Then the housing management service provider will form a management body of multi-family housing, appoint the head of the management office to serve as the representative of the management body, and mobilize the technical personnel and equipment necessary for the management of the multi-family housing.

Management work to be conducted by the head of the management office and technical personnel includes the management of common areas in multi-family housing and the implementation of resolutions made by the council of occupants' representatives. In fact, there is no difference between autonomous management and entrusted management in terms of the scope, methods, and difficulty of the work to be conducted by the management body of multi-family housing. However, a significant difference exists with regard to the party that organizes the management body. In the case of entrusted management, a housing management service provider, instead of a council of occupants' representatives, hires the head of the management office (the representative of the management body of multi-family housing) and technical personnel and signs an employment agreement with them, therefore requiring no employment relationship to be established between the council of occupants' representatives and workers including the head of the management office and technical personnel. Depending on the management method, the status of the head of the management office and technical personnel and their recourse to disciplinary actions such as unfair dismissal will vary.

4) Status and organization of a council of occupants' representatives

Occupants, etc. living in multi-family housing (occupants and users) shall elect a person who will represent their multi-family housing unit (building) as the representative of each building. Subsequently, the council of occupants' representatives is organized as an autonomous group consisting of the representatives of different buildings as council members. The council members then elect the executive officers of the council (chairperson, directors, and auditors) among themselves.

The council of occupants' representatives is an autonomous organization that represents occupants, etc. and has the authority to determine various matters related to the management of multi-family housing. Therefore, membership of the council is an important issue for occupants, etc. Pursuant to the Multi-Family Housing Management Act, only occupants are eligible to run for election, while the right to vote is granted to both occupants and users.

With regard to organizing the council of occupants' representatives, it is difficult for representatives in full-time employment to examine various issues relating to the management of multi-family housing and attend various meetings. In such cases, organizing the council is not easy, and the failure to organize the council may result in problems including the inability to decide upon important matters such as the selection of subcontractors for the management of multi-family housing and the execution of management expenses. On the other hand, there are cases where representatives serve prolonged terms, receiving money in exchange for certain privileges or processing managerial work by illicitly using their status and authority. To prevent such cases, recent amendments of the Multi-Family Housing Management Act added provisions on the following: 1. the exceptional expansion of eligibility to run for election; and 2. restriction on the term of office of representatives of each building. Specifically, the Act previously stipulated that, in principle, only occupants were eligible to run for election for representative of each building. The amendment stipulated that, if no occupant runs for the election, users who satisfy the qualification requirements shall also be eligible for the election. Furthermore, the Act restricted their term of office to two consecutive terms, with the aim to eliminate side effects that might occur from prolonged terms of office. However, if no occupant registers as a candidate in the election despite two notices, an occupant who is otherwise subject to the restriction on the term of office is allowed to register as a candidate in order to facilitate the organization of the council of occupants' representatives.

In addition, occupants, etc. may organize an election committee to deal with various affairs related to the election and dismissal of the representatives of each building and executive officers of the council of occupants' representatives.

5) Management rules

Management rules refer to rules of autonomy prescribed by occupants, etc. on the management or use of their multi-family housing. Management rules may be formulated or amended autonomously by occupants, etc. of the multi-family housing, while the head of the local government establishes standing rules for the management rules, which serve as the criteria for the management or use of multi-family housing to protect the occupants, etc. of multi-family housing and to maintain an orderly residential life. Occupants, etc. establish management rules in accordance with the standing rules.

In general, the management rules deal with the following matters in a comprehensive manner: rights and obligations of occupants, etc.; organization and operation of the council of occupants' representatives; election procedures, grounds for dismissal, and dismissal procedures for the representative of each building; organization and operation of the election committee; organization and operation of the management body of multi-family housing; methods to access materials prepared and maintained by the council of occupants' representatives or management entity; entrusted management contracts; procedures for the collection, safekeeping and usage of management expenses, etc.; long-term repair rates and procedure of using reserves for long-term repairs; auditing; and revitalization of community life.

6) Business entities' warranty liability for defects

There are cases where a business entity constructs multi-family housing and sells it to ordinary people, and then defects are found in the housing. In anticipation of such cases, the Multi-Family Housing Management Act prescribes that the business entity shall put down a security deposit with a financial institution, etc. for the purpose of repairing defects during the period of warranty liability to guarantee the repair of defects, or purchase a guarantee product that guarantees the payment of the security deposit for repairing defects, as prescribed by the applicable law.

In cases where any defects are discovered during the warranty liability period, the council of occupants' representatives, etc. may make a claim for the repair of the defects with the business entity. If the business entity has an objection to the claim made by the council of occupants' representatives, etc., the business entity, in consultation with the council of occupants' representatives, etc. may request a safety inspection entity to examine the defects to verify whether the defects are subject to the warranty liability, as prescribed by the applicable law. The government has established the Defect Examination and Dispute Mediation Committee to examine defects and mediate disputes about warranty liability for defects.

7) Central and local government support for the management of multi-family housing

As discussed above, the government has established the Defect Examination and Dispute Mediation Committee to examine defects and mediate disputes over defects, while local governments have formulated standing rules for management rules. Along with such activities, central and local governments provide support for the management of multi-family housing.

The central government has designated specific institutions or organizations as an "organization supporting the management of multi-family housing" to provide consultation on civil affairs and education related to the management of multi-family housing, offer support for the establishment and amendment of the management rules, and assist other affairs related to the management of multi-family housing.

To increase the transparency and efficiency of multi-family housing management, the government has also established and operates the "multi-family housing management information system," which enables comprehensive management of information on multi-family housing management. In addition, the government delivers various kinds of education and training including education for members, etc. of the council of occupants' representatives, education for the adjustment of the long-term repair plan, and firefighting safety education. However, the sub-tasks of such activities are entrusted to relevant organizations.

The head of the local government may request occupants, etc., the council of occupants' representatives and its members, the management entity, the head of the management office, etc. to submit materials or issue other necessary orders, and examine and inspect facilities, ledgers, and documents in relation to the multi-family housing, in order to boost the efficiency of multi-family housing management and protect occupants, etc. To this end, local governments may exercise the authority to oversee the management of multi-family housing and impose a fine when any breach is found.

4. Conclusion

In this chapter, the management system for multi-family housing was examined with a focus on the key stipulations of the Multi-Family Housing Management Act. This management system is considered to have been established and developed over decades to reflect various factors, including the supply of multi-family housing, occupants' economic and social situations and their awareness thereof, fostering of specialists in the management of multi-family housing, and support from the central and local governments. Currently, the management system is gradually being enhanced by synthesizing and reflecting opinions of society members to address real challenges with regard to the management of multi-family housing including difficulties in organizing a council of occupants' representatives, disputes among multi-family housing stakeholders such as occupants, etc., council of occupants' representatives, and management entities, inefficient and opaque management of multi-family housing, and conflicts regarding the financial burden of expenses for the management of multi-family housing.

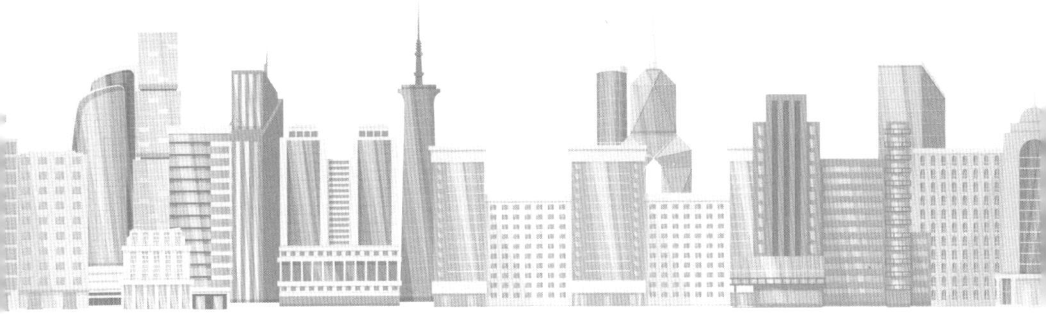

CHAPTER 4

Qualification System and Expertise of Housing Managers

CHAPTER 4

Qualification System and Expertise of Housing Managers

Ah-Rim Ahn,
Senior Researcher of the Korea Research Institute of Housing Management

1. Introduction of the housing manager qualification system and the assignment of housing managers

1) Background and development history of the housing manager qualification system

During the 1950s and 1960s, the government dedicated its utmost efforts to supplying high-density multi-family housing in order to efficiently ease the housing shortage within a short period of time. Thanks to the government's efforts to supply high-rise, concentrated multi-family housing, the number of multi-family housing increased rapidly. However, as problems caused by flimsy construction were often found, the importance of management started to be recognized. In particular, the fatal collapse of the Wawoo Apartment in Mapo-gu on April 8, 1970 served to bring greater attention to the management of multi-family housing.

Under these circumstances, a housing manager system was established through the amendment of the Housing Construction Promotion Act in December 1977, and two years later, the qualification criteria for housing managers were defined and announced through the Decree on Multi-Family Housing Management. However, as the qualification criteria only covered matters on management personnel and facilities, it was evaluated to be insufficient to guarantee expertise in management affairs (Ha et al., 2014).

The system of awarding qualification through examinations was detailed when the amended Housing Construction Promotion Act prescribed matters on housing managers' roles, qualification exams, disqualification, and required education in 1987. The qualification exam was first administered in 1990, three years after the housing manager qualification system was legislated, and in 1997, the government started to obligatorily assign housing management specialists selected through the qualification exam.

When the government assigned mandatory housing managers to multi-family housing, it targeted housing with 300 or more households, elevators, or a central heating system.[1] However, the regulation has partially changed in 1988 to only assign housing managers to multi-family housing with elevators or a central heating system when it accommodates more than 150 households.[2]

In the late 2000s, various types of multi-family housing emerged and resulted in some management problems with multi-family housing that is not subject to the obligatory assignment of housing managers.[3] To address management issues arising from multi-family housing that is not subject to compulsory management, the government tightened the relevant regulation in 2008 so that the obligatory assignment of housing managers was also applied to multipurpose residential buildings with 150 or more households. In 2010, the government applied the same conditions to rental apartment houses and mandated that all rental apartments should also employ housing managers. This expansion of the scope of multi-family housing subject to compulsory management contributed to broadening housing managers' work scope and increasing the demand for the certificate of

1 Decree on Multi-Family Housing Management (started to take effect on July 10, 1997)

2 Decree on Multi-Family Housing Management (started to take effect on December 31, 1998)

3 Multi-family housing that is not subject to compulsory management

qualification for housing managers.

In addition to the expansion of the application scope, housing managers became entitled to work as a general disaster manager in 2013 under the Enforcement Rules of the Special Act on Management of Disasters in Super High-rise Buildings and Complex Buildings with Underground Connections. With the increasing importance of housing management, housing managers' work scope has been steadily expanding.

Currently, multi-family housing that falls under any of the following is designated as "multi-family housing subject to compulsory management," which is also obliged to employ housing managers in accordance with the Multi-Family Housing Management Act.

1. Multi-family housing with 300 or more households
2. Multi-family housing with 150 or more households and with elevators installed
3. Multi-family housing with 150 or more households and with a central heating system (including a district heating system) installed
4. A building that consists of housing with 150 or more households and facilities other than housing[4]

Figure 1 Development history of the housing manager system

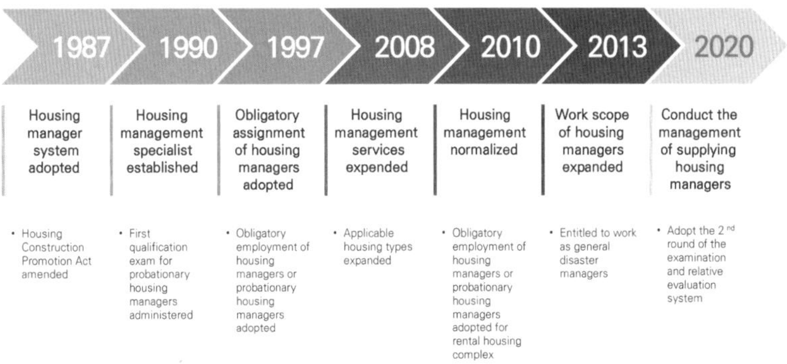

Source: Ha et al. (2014).

4 Refers to a multipurpose residential building with space for residential use, where at least 150 households reside

2) Qualification criteria and assignment of housing managers

Housing managers assigned to multi-family housing are divided into housing managers and probationary housing managers. A person who has passed the applicable qualification exam acquires a qualification as a probationary housing manager. However, even with the qualification, it does not mean that the qualified person can work as the head of a management office at every multi-family housing. Probationary housing managers can work as the head of the management office at multi-family housing with fewer than 500 households, and as an assistant to the head of the management office at multi-family housing with 500 or more households.[5] To work as the head of the management office at multi-family housing with at least 500 households, they must possess a housing manager qualification with relevant work experience.[6]

The housing manager qualification system was intended primarily for field workers passing the applicable qualification exam and with a set amount of relevant experience, under the aim to produce experts with a significant experience and knowhow. To achieve this objective, in the

5 Article 64 of the Multi-Family Housing Management Act, Article 69 of the Enforcement Decree of the Multi-Family Housing Management Act

6 Currently, a person who has a probationary housing manager qualification and meets any of the following requirements is recognized to be qualified as a housing manager (Article 73(1) of the Enforcement Decree of the Multi-Family Housing Management Act).

1. At least three years' work experience as the head of the management office of multi-family housing with at least 50 and fewer than 500 households
2. At least five years' experience in housing management affairs as an employee (excluding guards, cleaners and disinfectors) of the management office of multi-family housing with at least 50 households or as an employee of a housing management service provider
3. At least five years' experience in housing management affairs as an employee of the Korea Land and Housing Corporation or a local public company
4. At least five years' experience in affairs concerning guidance and supervision and approval and permission related to housing as a public official
5. At least five years' experience in affairs related to housing as an executive officer or an employee of an organization of housing managers and an organization related to the management of multi-family housing prescribed and announced by the Minister of Land, Infrastructure and Transport
6. At least five years' total work experience under subparagraphs 1 through 5

early stage of its adoption, the system mandated that housing managers should also take a separate examination. However, this idea was not implemented and the qualification system continues to grant qualifications according to years of relevant work experience.

The qualification exam for housing managers consists of two rounds. The first round of the examination deals with accounting principles, introduction of multi-family housing facilities, and the Civil Act, while the second round covers applicable laws on housing management and business practices in the management of multi-family housing. The related laws include the Housing Act, Multi-Family Housing Management Act, Special Act on Private Rental Housing, Special Act on Public Housing, Building Act, Special Act on the Safety Control and Maintenance of Establishments, Framework Act on Fire-fighting Services, Electric Utility Act, Elevator Facilities Safety Management Act, and Act on Ownership and Management of Condominium Buildings. Business practices in the management of multi-family housing deals with highly specific details.

Meanwhile, the authority to assign a housing manager as the head of a management office is granted to the council of occupants' representatives, housing management service provider, rental business operator, and business entity before the transfer of managerial affairs.[7] According to data from the Korea Housing Managers Association, which is a statutory organization, the number of housing managers and probationary housing managers who have reported their assignment and are working as the head of a management office are 11,361 and 2,004, respectively.[8] In total, at least 13,000 housing managers and probationary housing managers are working as the head of a management office.[9]

7 Transfer of management affairs is performed in accordance with Article 13(1) of the Multi-Family Housing Management Act.

8 Membership management system of the Korea Housing Managers Association (as of May 29, 2019)

9 For multi-family housing that is not subject to compulsory management, it is not mandatory to report the assignment of a housing manager. Considering that there are housing managers and probationary housing managers assigned to multi-family housing that is not subject to compulsory management, there are likely to be more

2. Work and expertise of housing managers

1) Key tasks of housing managers

A housing manager assigned as the head of a management office conducts a wide range of work. The work is largely divided into operational management (administrative control), maintenance (technical management), and everyday management (welfare management). This generalized division of work may make the work of housing managers appear to be simple. However, upon closer inspection, it becomes apparent that the scope of their work is fairly broad. Operational management work includes management affairs in the areas of accounting, administrative work, human resources, occupants, public relations, and welfare facilities. Maintenance work covers environment, buildings, safety, and facilities management. Lastly, eve management work encompasses affairs concerning community culture, community revitalization, and social welfare. As such, housing managers deal with a vast range of work from conserving the value of multi-family housing's assets to management work for occupants. For example, the head of the management office is responsible for the adjustment of the safety management plan, business support and work processing necessary for operating the council of occupants' representatives and election committee, provision of information on multi-family housing, responses against any violation, responses to safety accidents, thefts, and other incidents, and claim for repairing defects by proxy.

Although the head of the management office conducts a vast range of work, the decision-making authority is retained by the council of occupants' representatives, and therefore, when expenditure is required, the head of the management office must follow the relevant decision made by the council. In other words, the head of the management office may

housing managers and probationary housing managers working as the head of a management office.

not spend expenses at his/her sole discretion. In addition, the authority to make decisions on a number of issues concerning the management of multi-family housing is not given to the head of the management office, which sometimes causes problems.

Figure 2 Key tasks of housing managers

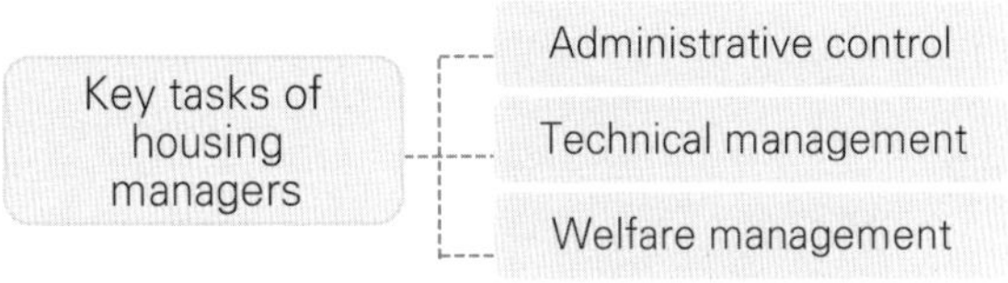

2) Expertise of housing management work

To work as the head of a management office, housing managers should receive placement training, supplementary training, and other necessary training. The content of training should include laws applicable to managers, knowledge and ethics required of managers, technical skills such as methods of replacing and repairing important facilities, defect repair procedures, and dispute resolution.

Figure 3 Housing manager training

Source: Korea Housing Managers Association (2019).

Compulsory education prescribed by law for housing managers deals with practical matters required for conducting housing management work.

The education is usually entrusted to institutions selected by the City Mayor or Province Governor and currently, the Korea Housing Managers Association provides a significant part of the education.

Figure 4 Korea Housing Managers Association Website

Source: Korea Housing Managers Association (2019).

The below table outlines some of the compulsory education offered by the Korea Housing Managers Association. Placement training is separated between housing managers and probationary housing managers because their job performance may differ depending on the work experience. Placement training for housing managers includes more detailed practical affairs than training for probationary housing managers.

Table 1 Compulsory education (subject to a fine for incompletion)

Course (hours)	Trainee	Subject
Placement (pre-placement) training concerning the management of multi-family housing and ethics, for probationary housing managers (including preliminary education and refresher course) (Three days (20 hours))*	A probationary housing manager who intends to be assigned as the head of a management office for the first time A person who has been assigned less than a year ago	Key content of the Multi-Family Housing Management Act and other laws on housing management Ethics and knowledge necessary for prospective housing managers Labor management

	A person who has no relevant career experience within the past five years from the scheduled date of assignment	Establishment, review, enforcement, etc. of long-term repair plan Facility safety and inspection Management rules and responses to civil complaints Accounting standards Guidelines for selecting a subcontractor in a bid
Placement training concerning the management of multi-family housing and ethics, for housing managers (including preliminary education and refresher course) (Three days (20 hours))*	A person who has acquired a housing manager qualification while working as the head of a management office and where the date of acquiring the qualification is less than a year ago A person who has no relevant career experience within the past five years from the scheduled date of assignment	Key content of the Multi-Family Housing Management Act and other laws on housing management Ethics and knowledge required of the head of a management office Communication within multi-family housing and responses to power abuse Auditing Implementation of repair work Practical affairs concerning the operation of the council of occupants' representatives Cases of responses to civil complaints Bidding and contracts
Supplementary training concerning the management of multi-family housing and ethics, for housing managers (probationary housing managers) (Three days (20 hours))*	A person who has completed placement training or supplementary training for housing managers (probationary housing managers) less than three years (36 months) ago	Practical affairs concerning the order placement of construction work Inspection and evaluation of structures Cases of responses to civil

		affairs Bidding and contracts Legal affairs (management rules and representation of lawsuit) Bidding
Facility safety education (One day (four hours) x two times (first half and second half))**	A person responsible for facility safety management listed in the facility safety management plan for multi-family housing subject to compulsory management (selected among management staff)	Overview of the safety management of multi-family housing facilities, and history management Safety management of mechanical facilities including water supply, heating, and firefighting facilities Safety management of children's playgrounds
Education for the establishment and adjustment of long-term repair plan (One day (eight hours) for each: practice course and computer practice course)***	The head of the management office assigned to multi-family housing with 300 or more households, with elevators installed, or with a district heating system adopted	Laws on the operation of the long-term repair plan Operation and review of the long-term repair plan Cases of responding to questions about the long-term repair plan Examples of quantity estimation for a standard complex User manual for the long-term repair plan operating system

**Note: Pursuant to Article 70 of the Multi-Family Housing Management Act*
***Note: Pursuant to Article 32 of the Multi-Family Housing Management Act*
****Note: Pursuant to Article 29 of the Multi-Family Housing Management Act*

(Table 2) Optional education (not subject to a fine for incompletion)

Course (hours)	Trainee	Subject
Safety inspection education* for housing managers (Five days (35 hours))	A person who wishes to conduct a safety inspection under Article 33(1) of the Multi-Family Housing Management Act, and who has been assigned or intends to be assigned as the head of a management office after acquiring a housing manager qualification (or a probationary housing manager qualification), or who has been working or intends to work as management staff	Explanation on the applicable laws and guidelines Practical affairs concerning preliminary and on-site surveys Characteristics of the materials of structures and facilities Electric equipment in multi-family housing Roles and responsibilities of electrical safety managers Understanding of design books, on-site survey skills and practice, etc.
Regular safety and health education** for management supervisors (One day (eight hours) x two times (first half and second half)***)	A person who works for multi-family housing in the management supervisor position (who directs and supervises practical affairs regardless of the position)	Introduction to occupational safety and health including prevention of industrial accidents Prevention of health issues among customer service employees Safety and health among building management service providers Risk assessment and practice in the building management business

**Note: Pursuant to Article 33(1) of the Multi-Family Housing Management Act*

***Note: Pursuant to Article 31 of the Occupational Safety and Health Act and Article 33 of the Enforcement Rules of the same Act*

****Note: Workplaces with no industrial accidents in the past year may take only one course (eight hours) of their choice.*

3. Improvement of the qualification system for housing managers

1) Enhancement of expertise

Currently, prospective housing managers prepare for the qualification exam at a private education institute. In preparing for the exam, they gain the knowledge required to be qualified as housing managers. However, in addition to specialized knowledge on multi-family housing, relevant expertise developed based on significant practical experience is crucial to effective management. This is because housing managers are responsible for a wide range of work, from affairs that require specialized knowledge such as the safety management of multi-family housing facilities to community management such as promoting smooth communication with occupants and resolving civil complaints.

The expertise of housing managers can be enhanced in several ways, for example, by creating a curriculum for housing management-related studies, expanding the qualification verification procedure, and guaranteeing their status as housing managers. First, with regard to the curriculum for housing management, it may be a viable option to create a housing management department at a lifelong education center or a technical college to provide students with sufficient theoretical and practical education before acquiring qualifications for housing management.

Second is to intensify the qualification verification procedure. Work experience is not an infallible proof of qualification as a housing manager. To enhance the recognition of the housing manager qualification as a guarantee of expertise in housing management, additional verification tools are required, including intensive training or qualification exams. The expertise of housing managers is directly related to the residential stability of the general public. Currently, only housing managers who work as the head of a management office are obligated to complete relevant education and training, while it is not mandatory for housing managers to receive education unless working as the head of a management office. Therefore, if a person has passed the qualification exam 10 years ago but has never worked as the head of a management office, he/she is not obligated to complete the required education, but once assigned as the head of a management office, he/she should complete the required education within a year from the start of employment. However, as the service period of the head of a management office is less than a year in many cases, there is a need to consider measures to supplement the education system.

Third, a guarantee of the status of housing managers as the head of a management office is associated with work continuity and accountability. According to the 2014 survey on the current management status of "clean apartments" in Seoul presented in the report on the "Study of Measures to Advance Multi-Family Housing Management (Park et al., 2015)," service periods of heads of management offices at five apartment complexes ranged from four to seven months. This frequent turnover among the heads of management offices may compromise work continuity and lead to negligence in management work such as the evasion of accountability. If employment for a certain period of time is guaranteed, and terms of dismissal as a result of negligence are established so as to prevent the side effects of the guarantee of the employment period, it will contribute to enhancing the expertise of housing managers as the head of a management office.

2) Improvement of housing managers' status and treatment

One of the important roles of housing managers is communicating with occupants to deal with civil complaints such as inconveniences experienced by occupants in the apartment community. As the authority to assign housing managers as the head of the management office is held by the council of occupants' representatives (under the autonomous management system), the head of the management office is subordinate to the council in most cases. This hierarchy often forces the head of the management office to endure unfair treatment or unreasonable orders.

According to a case study of unreasonable interference or inappropriate instructions (Kang et al., 2018), over 90% of the cases of unreasonable interference were found to have not been reported or requested to be investigated.[10] Despite the legal stipulation that "where the council of occupants' representatives causes or is likely to cause losses to occupants, etc. through its unreasonable interference in the head of the management office performing duties, the head of the management office may report the fact to the head of a *Si/Gun/Gu* and request him/her to make an examination of the fact," only very few cases have been reported in reality. The majority of the respondents (58.9%) cited the "fear of retaliation or disadvantages in relation to work performance or human resources affairs" as a reason.

Considering the study results, guaranteeing the status of housing managers to enhance their expertise may also contribute to improving their treatment. The guarantee of housing managers' status will enable them to demand the correction or investigation of problematic situations while demonstrating their competence as experts with strong conviction and willpower.

As for professionals with appropriate qualifications such as licensed real estate agents and certified appraisers, there are applicable laws in place. However, legal support for housing managers remains insufficient. Therefore, it may be an effective alternative to enact legislation on housing managers to establish housing managers as an independent position, thus contributing to the expansion of management services for occupants.

10 Found to be 91.5% in 2016 and 93.2% in 2017

References

Kang, E. T., Choi, T. G., & Ahn, A. R. (2018). A Case Study of Unreasonable Interference and Inappropriate Instructions. Korea Research Institute of Housing Management.

Park, S. Y. et al. (2015). Measures to Advance Multi-Family Housing Management. Korea Center for City and Environment Research.

Ha, S. K. et al. (2014). *Contemporary Multifamily Housing Management: Theory and Practice*. Seoul: Parkyoungsa.

Korea Housing Managers Association. (2019). Statistics of Successful Applicants of the Qualification Exam for Housing Managers section on the website of the Korea Housing Managers Association. Retrieved from http://www.khma.org/portal/00007/00016/00029.web. (Accessed on May 2, 2019)

Korea Housing Managers Association. (2019). List of Workers. Membership Management System of the Korea Housing Managers Association. Internal Data. (Accessed on May 28, 2019)

CHAPTER 5

Management Expenses and Reserves for Long-term Repairs in Multi-Family Housing

CHAPTER 5

Management Expenses and Reserves for Long-term Repairs in Multi-Family Housing

Eun-Taek Kang,
Senior Researcher of the Korea Research Institute of Housing Management

1. What are multi-family housing management expenses?

1) Definition and items of management expenses

Management expenses are operated and used to build a pleasant residential environment and to benefit occupants. Management expenses are paid by occupants and divided into common management fees and user fees.

Common management fees consist of 10 items in total: fees for general management, cleaning, security, disinfection, elevator maintenance, maintenance of smart home network facilities, heating, hot water supply, repair and maintenance, and entrusted management. Specifically, general management fees cover labor costs, office expenses, taxes and public utilities charges, clothing expenses, education and training fees, vehicle maintenance fees, and other expenses, while entrusted management fees are charged only when the management of the multi-family housing is entrusted to a housing management service provider. The usage of each item of common management fees and details are as shown in the following table.

Figure 1 Items of management expenses

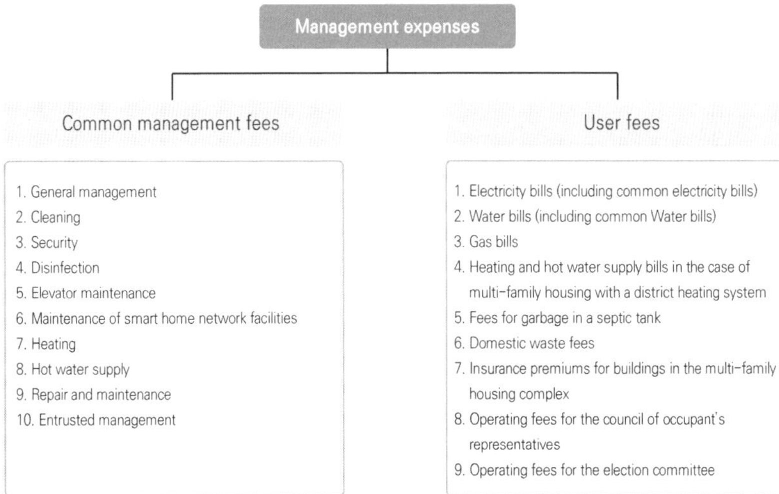

Table 1 Items of common management fees and their usage

Item	Usage
1. General management	A. Labor costs: Salaries, allowances, bonuses, severance pay, occupational health and safety insurance premiums, unemployment insurance premiums, national pension, health insurance premiums, and benefits including meal expenses B. Office expenses: Expenses directly incurred in conducting management affairs such as expenses for office supplies, books and printing, transportation and communications C. Taxes and public utilities charges: Electricity bills, communication fees, and postage fees incurred by management entities and taxes imposed on management entities, etc. D. Clothing expenses E. Education and training fees F. Vehicle maintenance fees: Fees directly incurred for vehicle maintenance such as fuel costs, repair fees, and car insurance premiums G. Other expenses: Expenses for the purchase of management supplies, auditing, and other expenses involving management affairs
2. Cleaning	When entrusted, entrustment fees; when directly operated, expenses directly incurred for cleaning such as cleaners'

	labor cost, clothing expenses, and cleaning supplies expenses
3. Security	When entrusted, entrustment fees; when directly operated, expenses directly incurred for security such as guards' labor costs and clothing expenses
4. Disinfection	When entrusted, entrustment fees; when directly operated, expenses directly incurred for disinfection such as disinfection supplies costs
5. Elevator maintenance	When entrusted, entrustment fees; when directly operated, incidental expenses, material cost, etc. However, electricity bills for elevators are included in the electricity bills of common facilities.
6. Maintenance of smart home network facilities	When entrusted, entrustment fees; when directly operated, expenses directly incurred for the maintenance and management of smart home network facilities such as labor costs in relation to smart home network facilities and material costs. However, relevant electricity bill is included in the electricity bills of common facilities.
7. Heating	Expenses after deducting hot water supply fees from costs for heating and hot water supply (gas bills, heating bills, and water costs for hot water supply)
8. Hot water supply	Gas bill and water cost for hot water supply
9. Repair and maintenance	A. Expenses incurred in repair and maintenance for common areas of multi-family housing that are not subject to the long-term repair plan under Article 29(1) of the Multi-Family Housing Management Act. When entrusted, entrustment fees; when directly operated, material costs and labor costs B. Maintenance and inspection fees for common facilities, such as expenses for cleaning heating and air-conditioning facilities and recharging fire extinguishers C. Safety inspection fees for buildings D. Expenses incurred to prevent disasters and accidents
10. Entrusted management	Monthly bill determined by the contract between the council of occupants' representatives and the housing management service provider, when management work is entrusted to a housing management service provider

Source: Appendix 2 of the Enforcement Decree of the Multi-Family Housing Management Act

Next, user fees refer to expenses incurred by occupants and included in the management expenses by the management entity. The management entity first collects the fees from the applicable occupants and then pays them to relevant entities. User fees include electricity, water supply, and gas bills, and heating and hot water supply bills in the case of a district heating system, fees for garbage in a septic tank, domestic waste fees, insurance premiums for buildings in the multi-family housing complex, fees for operating the council of occupants' representatives, and fees for operating the election committee.

2) Calculation and disclosure of management expenses

There are two methods of calculating management expenses: annual budgeting and monthly settlement. With the annual budgeting method, the total expenses estimated for a year are divided by the total supplied area of the housing and by 12 months, and then the resulting amount is multiplied by the supplied area of each household, thereby setting the monthly rate. On the other hand, in the monthly settlement system, the actual expenses incurred during the month are calculated by item and divided by the total supplied area of the housing and then the resulting amount is multiplied by the supplied area of each household. Most multi-family housing employ the latter method.

There are also several ways to charge management expenses: charging equal management expenses, charging in proportion to the area of each household, and charging in proportion to usage. In principle, management expenses should be charged according to the supplied area or usage of each household.

Currently, the multi-family housing management information system (http://www.k-apt.go.kr) publicly discloses the management expenses of multi-family housing subject to compulsory management, as part of efforts to promote the transparent use of management expenses.

Figure 2 The multi-family housing management information system

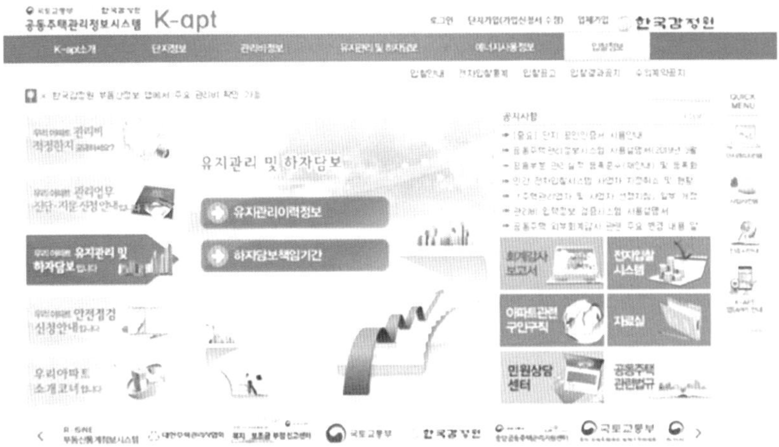

2. Current status of multi-family housing management expenses

1) Management expenses per year

The number of households and exclusive residential area of multi-family housing subject to compulsory management continue to increase. Meanwhile, common management fees per area are found to have increased steadily, whereas user fees per area have declined slightly.

As of 2018, the total monthly management expenses of a household with $80m^2$ of exclusive residential area are expected to be approximately 164,000 won, which consists of monthly common management fees ($1,024 \times 80m^2$ = 81,920 won) and user fees ($1,026 \times 80m^2$ = 82,080 won).

The total amount of management expenses of multi-family housing subject to compulsory management is found to have increased from about 14 trillion won in 2013 to about 18 trillion won in 2018.

Table 2 Average monthly management expenses of multi-family housing subject to compulsory management

Item	2013	2014	2015	2016	2017	2018
No. of households	7,833,107	8,148,518	8,406,033	8,708,338	9,088,041	9,552,865
Exclusive residential area (m^2)	597,993,189	621,905,767	641,315,050	662,874,927	690,284,252	725,287,278
Common management fees (won/m^2)	820	854	894	928	965	1,024
User fees (won/m^2)	1,157	1,093	1,085	1,063	1,007	1,026
Management expenses (won/m^2)	1,977	1,947	1,979	1,991	1,972	2,050

Source: Multi-family housing management information system (http://www.k-apt.go.kr)

Figure 3 Total amounts of management expenses of multi-family housing subject to compulsory management (unit: 100 million won)

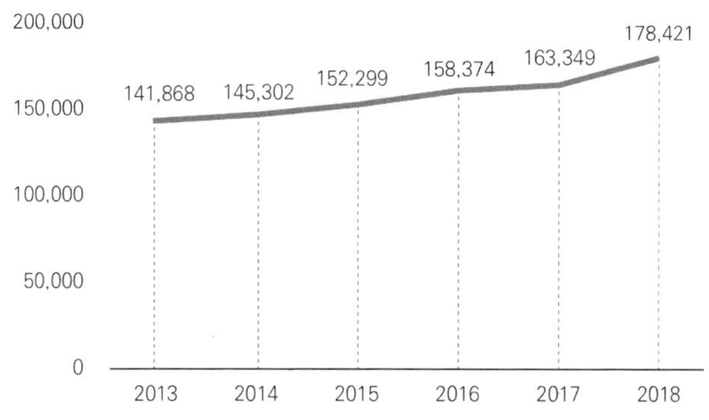

2) Management expenses per item

Items of common management fees and user fees are as follows. First, general management expenses were found to account for the largest share of the common management fees, followed by security, cleaning, and repair and maintenance expenses, in descending order. Specifically, general management, security, and cleaning expenses, which include labor costs for management office personnel, guards, and cleaners, respectively, were found to have a higher share, indicating that labor costs have a significant effect on common management fees.

Next, electricity bills occupy the largest share of user fees followed by water, heating, and hot water supply bills, in descending order. Electricity bills include common electricity bills incurred for the use of elevators, basement parking lots, senior citizen centers, etc. as well as individual electricity bills.

Table 3 Management expenses per item

Item		Average (won/m²)	Percentage (%)
Common management fees	General management	409	40.0
	Cleaning	172	16.8
	Security	332	32.5
	Disinfection	7	0.7
	Elevator maintenance	30	2.9
	Maintenance of smart home network facilities	2	0.2
	Repair and maintenance	64	6.3
	Entrusted management	7	0.7
	Sum	1,024	100.0
User fees	Heating	156	15.2
	Hot water supply	77	7.5
	Gas	2	0.2
	Electricity	530	51.6
	Water	220	21.4
	Garbage in the septic tank	2	0.2
	Domestic waste	12	1.2
	Operation of the council of occupants' representatives	13	1.3
	Premiums for buildings	13	1.3
	Operation of the election committee	2	0.2
	Sum	1.026	100.0

Source: Multi-family housing management information system (http://www.k-apt.go.kr)

3. Reserves for long-term repairs

1) Definition of reserves for long-term repairs and relevant items

To maintain multi-family housing as a pleasant and safe space and to conserve its value as a precious household asset, it is required to conduct safety inspections, planned maintenance, and ordinary repairs on an ongoing basis. To this end, establishing a long-term repair plan, accumulating reserves for long-term repairs under the plan, and implementing planned repairs are important measures to extend the life of buildings (Park et al., 2013). A long-term repair plan refers to an extended plan for the replacement and repair of key facilities to ensure the safe and efficient use of multi-family housing for a long period, and reserves for long-term repairs refer to money required according to the long-term repair plan, which is collected from the owners of the multi-family housing and then accumulated. Long-term repair fees are charged on the owners of the multi-family housing and operated separately from management expenses.

In the early stage of the reserve system, reserves for long-term repairs were accumulated for the purpose of replacing and repairing main facilities, but recently, its focus is shifting toward planned management for multi-family housing, so reserves are accumulated to replace and repair important facilities, ultimately to ensure the safe and efficient use of multi-family housing in the long run. Just as human beings receive periodic medical checkups and relevant treatments, multi-family housing also requires preemptive checks and regular planned repairs.

The items of a long-term repair plan are as shown in Table 4.

Table 4 Items subject to a long-term repair plan

Category	Item	
1. Exterior	Roofs Exterior windows and doors	Exterior
2. Interior	Ceilings Floors	Interior walls Stairs
3. Electric, firefighting, elevator, and smart home network facilities	Standby power sources (self-generation system) Automatic smoke detectors Elevators and hoists Communications and broadcasting facilities Security and crime prevention facilities	Substations Firefighting facilities Lightning arrester equipment, outdoor lights, etc. Boiler rooms and equipment rooms Smart home network facilities
4. Water supply, gas, drainage, and ventilation facilities	Water supply facilities Drains	Gas facilities Ventilation facilities
5. Heating and hot water supply facilities	Heating facilities	Hot water supply facilities
6. Outdoor auxiliary facilities and outdoor welfare facilities	Asphalt pavement, fences, kids' clubs, paved sidewalks, septic tanks, drains and manholes, roofs installed at the entrance and the approach space to the parking lot, bicycle racks, barrier gates, landscape facilities, signage	

Source: Appendix 1 of the Enforcement Rules of the Multi-Family Housing Management Act

2) Current status of reserves for long-term repairs

In principle, the calculation of reserves for long-term repairs follows the formula established by the Enforcement Rules of the Multi-Family Housing Management Act. However, most multi-family housing do not have sufficient reserves necessary for long-term repairs and maintenance.

$$\text{Monthly charge for long-term repairs per household} = \frac{\text{Total repair fees estimated for the period of the long-term repair plan}}{\text{Total supplied area} \times 12 \times \text{planned period(years)}} \times \text{supplied area of each household}$$

As shown in the below figure, monthly charges for long-term repairs have increased from 115 won/m^2 in 2013 to 153 won/m^2 in 2018. As of

2018, the monthly charge for long-term repairs for a household with a supplied area of 80m^2 was approximately 12,240 won.

(Figure 4) Monthly charge for long-term repairs (won/m^2)

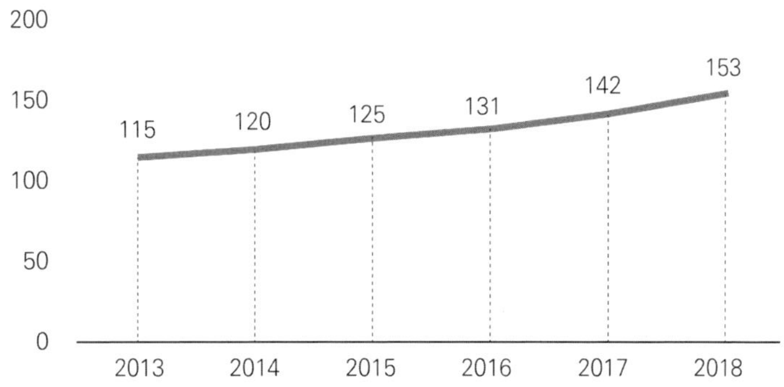

Reference

Park, E. C. et al. (2013). A Study on the Improvement of the Long-term Repair Program for Multi-Family Housing and the Accumulation of Reserves for Long-term Repairs as a Fund. Seoul Metropolitan Government.

CHAPTER 6

Remaining Challenges for Korea's Multi-Family Housing Management System

CHAPTER 6

Remaining Challenges for Korea's Multi-Family Housing Management System

Ta-Kwan Choi,
Director of Planning and Coordination of the Korea Research Institute of Housing Management

1. Decrepit apartments and blind spots in management

Everything on earth is bound to deteriorate as time goes by. The same applies to infrastructure or buildings.

The average age of Koreans has reached 40.4 for the first time in 2015, and the median age is approximately 41 years of age. This indicates that Korea is expected to face the demographic cliff in the very near future. A bigger problem is that the aging phenomenon is not limited to the population. National infrastructure and buildings of various types are also entering the aging era.

It was in the 1970s when the social infrastructure of Korea started to be established in earnest. As many of these facilities were built in a short period of time, they are also deteriorating simultaneously. Among major large-scale infrastructure such as dams, roads, bridges, and railroads, the number of facilities aged over 30 years recorded 2,017 (10%) in 2014. However, this number is estimated to increase by more than twofold to 4,488 (22.2%) in a few years.

Apartments also grow old. Having been constructed and supplied at an unprecedented rate, apartments came to accommodate more than 10 million households in only half a century. As housing types became diversified to include tenement houses, multipurpose residential buildings, and officetels, around 70% of Koreans today live in multi-family housing.

Figure 1 The past and the present of the first New Towns

Note: Construction of first New Town in the 1990s (left) and its current state (right)
Source: Topic Images Inc.

While wealthy property owners were celebrating that "house prices rose by millions of won when they woke up each morning" in the late 1980s ([Figure 1]), ordinary people's dream of owning a house became unrealistically distant. The rich were jubilant, but the ordinary people became resentful.

In response, the government hurriedly announced the New Town plan: the first New Towns were built in Bundang and Ilsan and people started to move to the New Towns in 1991. Apartments built against this backdrop in Bundang, Ilsan, Pyeongchon, Sanbon, and Jung-dong will soon become around 30 years old. According to a survey conducted by a media outlet, as many as 300,000 apartment units in the first New Towns alone were built almost 30 years ago. It is estimated that the number of such aged apartment units will soon exceed 3 million nationwide (Lee, 2017).

Figure 2 An apartment not subject to compulsory management (left) and an apartment subject to compulsory management (right)

Considering only the year of construction when discussing the problems of decrepit apartments reflects a myopic mindset in resolving these issues. Serious problems are hidden in small-scale apartment complexes with fewer than 150 households. This is because the Multi-Family Housing Management Act, which is considered to be the final word on housing management, stipulates that the management of an apartment complex not subject to compulsory management should be left to autonomous management by the occupants of the multi-family housing, who are not experts.

The Multi-Family Housing Management Act stipulates in detail the management of buildings and facilities, regulations on accounting including management expenses, regulations on the operation of communities such as the council of occupants' representatives, and provisions regarding the assignment of housing managers. In particular, the long-term repair plan has a direct and significant impact on the lifespan of apartment buildings. Although the two apartment buildings in [Figure 2] are both 30 years old, the difference between the building subject to compulsory management (right, built in 1971, 1,790 households) and the building not subject to compulsory management (left, built in 1970, 130 households) is immediately noticeable at a glance. Complexes that are not managed properly saw the rapid growth of slums ([Figure 2]). In addition, urgent measures are required since decrepit small-scale complexes are mostly occupied by socially-disadvantaged demographics such as the poor, the elderly, and the disabled, as in the case of Apartment S in Yongsan-gu (left).

Even in cases where repairs are needed, small-scale apartment complexes do not possess the funds to fix the problem, which in turn causes a vicious circle whereby other parts break down more quickly. The amendment of the Act in 2019 added the non-mandatory provision stipulating that the occupants of apartment complexes with fewer than 150 households are eligible to receive specialized management if desired. However, it appears that the implementation of the said provision remains distant. This is because people are highly sensitive to management expenses in reality. However, the failure to dedicate sufficient funds to address problems could result in even more serious problems.

In terms of human residence, safety is the most important factor for improving the quality of life. If it is true that buildings also age in a certain order, we must discard the idea of putting a price on a long-range plan for the safety of old residential facilities.

2. Challenges faced by employees engaged in multi-family housing management

Incidents such as assault and power abuse over security guards working in apartment complexes continue to occur. Recently, a security guard in his 70s working at an apartment in Seoul was beaten by a drunken occupant and fell into a comatose state. In another incident in Suseong-gu, Daegu, in June 2018, an occupant attacked a security guard with a broom (Park, 2018).

Security Guard B at an apartment in Gangnam, Seoul poured gasoline over his body and set himself on fire at around 9 a.m. on October 7, 2014.

An occupant who witnessed the incident quickly doused the fire using a fire extinguisher, but Security Guard B suffered third-degree burns all over his body. Despite receiving more than 6,000 skin grafts and medical treatment in an intensive care unit, Security Guard B suffered multiple organ failures caused by sepsis and eventually died after a month of suffering.

Occupant C had instructed Security Guard B to clean up his food waste, and threw leftover cookies from the fifth floor and ordered the security guard to eat them off the ground.

In 2013, at Apartment H, which was considered one of the most troublesome apartments in Northern Gyeonggi-do, three occupants created a nuisance for the other 800 households, causing countless complaints and charges to be made. Kim, the head of the management office who was appointed at the request of the management company, had to visit the city hall and police station two or three times every week immediately following his appointment to the post. Occupants were unable to discern who is right or wrong for a prolonged period. Some occupants were swayed by the perpetrators who sought to foment friction, and even criticized Kim. While enduring abusive language, the use of physical force, and threats, while undergoing complex lawsuits, Kim began to suspect health issues, which he disregarded to prioritize his professional duties. After three years of struggle, the management of the apartment stabilized. However, due to the continuous build-up of stress, Kim collapsed at work a few months later and succumbed to his condition. He was only 41 years old (Kim, 2016).

It is urgent to ensure better treatment by law to employees engaged in multi-family housing management, as they work at the lowest rungs of the social ladder. At the same time, it is also necessary to change the mindset of occupants.

3. Multi-family housing, complex enough to legislate against unreasonable interference

Workers engaged in the management of multi-family housing include housing managers who work as the head of the management office; office clerks in charge of accounting, administration, civil affairs, etc.; facility staff in charge of maintenance and management of facilities; security guards in charge of safety; and cleaners in charge of the sanitation of the residential environment. They fulfil their own duties diligently in order for residents to enjoy a pleasant and happy residential life.

Numerous reports state that employees working for residents of multi-family housing suffer from assault, verbal abuse, and power abuse by the residents. According to a media report in 2018, a drunken occupant assaulted a security guard to death, simply because the security guard did not address his complaint about between-floor noise. Another occupant attacked the female head of the management office and the management department head for personal reasons, saying that they did not make a banner for the apartment as requested.

To rectify these problematic trends in multi-family housing management, Article 65 of the Multi-Family Housing Management Act stipulates the preclusion of unreasonable interference in the duties of the head of the management office and the prohibition of inappropriate instructions or orders to workers engaged in multi-family housing management beyond the scope of their duties.

According to "A Case Study of Unreasonable Interference and Inappropriate Instructions" conducted by the Korea Research Institute of Housing Management of the Korea Housing Managers Association, approximately 300,000 workers engaged in the residential and nonresidential property management business as of 2018 (Kang et al., 2018).

The rate of new housing supply has already exceeded 103.8% compared to that of year 2017. As the housing supply rate began to exceed 100%, the apartment market began to stabilize. As the focus was placed on stable residential life, occupants started to act like an employer (contract-giver), the ground of which is assumed to be represented in the form of a "power abuses."

Occupants, who had tightened their belts to buy their own houses in the past, are now desperately searching for a way to reduce management expenses, for example, by keenly observing apartment management employees. In other words, they interfere inappropriately under the pretense of highlighting management issues.

Figure 3 Percentage of employees who have experienced unreasonable interference

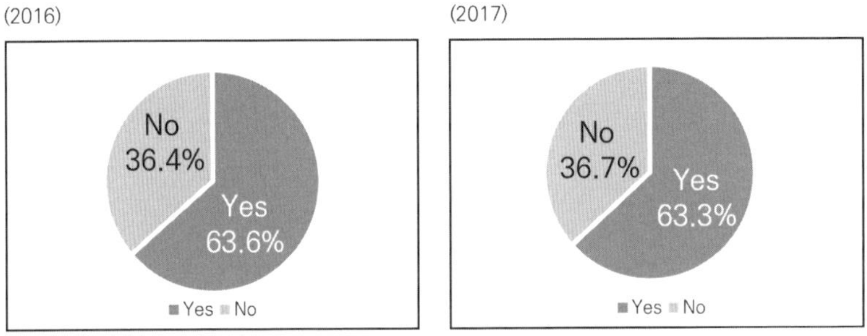

Source: Korea Research Institute of Housing Management(2018)

Although workers engaged in multi-family housing management face a working environment poorer than that of ordinary companies, power abuses over such workers have become widespread across society. In addition, occupants of multi-family housing make unreasonable requests to the head of the management office, female office clerks, security guards, cleaners and others, or insult their dignity, which frequently occur in the management of multi-family housing. Such power abuses have gone so far as to take someone's precious life. Most occupants remain uninterested in multi-family housing management, but in some apartments, management workers are being referred to as "companions" to encourage occupants to treat them as they would family.

Over time, unreasonable interference continues to occur at a rate of more than 60% as shown in [Figure 3]. This is due to the absence of regulations to punish perpetrators of power abuses. To improve this situation, it is necessary to revise the related laws.

4. The capacity of the head of the management office

The Article 64(2) of the Multi-Family Housing Management Act stipulates that "the head of the management office shall perform the following duties to protect the rights and interests of occupants, etc. of multi-family housing through the safe and efficient management of multi-family housing."

The head of the management office, hereinafter Manager G, persuaded the representative of each building to grant a contract to a subsidiary of the apartment's management company in a bid for security guard services, but ultimately failed. The chairperson of the council of occupants' representatives decided to grant the contract to a different company, saying, "I understand your situation, but let's go with Company A this time." Although the chairperson promised, "We have cleaning scheduled in two months. We can hire the company then," the chairperson once again chose a different company to conclude a contract in a bid for cleaning services several months later. Manager G was told by the management company that he was an "incompetent manager" (Kim, 2016).

As a result, it is likely that Manager G's name was placed on a blacklist among entrusted management companies.

Under the entrusted management system, the head of the management office inevitably assumes the role of a sales representative of the entrusted management company, rather than solely fulfilling the duties of a housing manager as a specialist in housing management. It has been a long time since this change in the role of the head of the management office took root in the system. As an entrusted management company is a private company, it does not recognize loyalty to the company if its employee does not contribute to the company's profits. However, as management services are provided for everyone in the complex and therefore constitute non-competitive and non-exclusive public goods (Ha et al., 2014), the resultant housing manager system has proven to require a professional role to ensure systematic and reasonable management. Nevertheless, the distorted operating method that forces specialists in housing management to take on the duties of a sales representative requires reform.

5. Problems of between-floor noise

A multi-family housing unit shares its ceilings, floors and walls with other units based on its building structure, which presents problems stemming from neighbors living in close contact. Among such problems, between-floor noise has emerged as a social issue. These noise problems occur continuously and lack a clear solution. The number of disputes and complaints among neighbors is increasing each year. As the damage and the number of disputes caused by the noise issue increased, the government presented the Guideline for the Prevention of Between-floor Noise. However, the guideline does not apply to multi-family housing constructed under a construction project plan that was approved prior to the enforcement of the applicable law (Jung, 2009).

There are three main causes of between-floor noise: human factors such as children running (73%) and hammering (4.7%); structural factors such as sounds of toilets flushing and doors opening and closing; and institutional factors that are instrumental in preventing and solving these problems. Human factors can be solved to a certain degree, but there are limitations for individuals to address the structural factors. The problems caused by structural factors are attributed to the fact that wall structure apartment buildings, which account for 85% of apartments in Korea, are not efficient in blocking outside noise (Lee, 2016).

Lee (2015) made a novel argument in "A Study on the Government's

Measures to Support for Solving Problems of Between-floor Noise in Multi-Family Housing." To summarize his findings, first, the cause of the between-floor noise lies in the fact that multi-family housing was constructed according to the Housing Act, which did not consider the noise caused by the residential environment. Primarily, the government is responsible for the noise issue, and secondarily, a housing culture of disregard toward others and the Korean floor heating system of *ondol* are to blame. Second, provisions on noise between floors stipulated in the current law should be amended from non-compulsory to compulsory provisions. Third, the reinforced Housing Act is not very effective in preventing heavy floor impact noises, which are responsible for 85% of between-floor noise. Therefore, the detailed provisions should be newly enacted to allow the management committee or management office to handle the problem appropriately by applying technology such as a noise management system.

Fourth, in responding to complaints filed with the Central Environmental Dispute Mediation Committee, Korea Environment Corporation, and local governments, providing one-on-one consulting does not present a fundamental solution and therefore such problems should be solved systematically by applying a management system that measures the noise in multi-family housing on an ongoing basis and allows the management office to monitor the noise. Fifth, the between-floor noise is already a subject of public interest, and the public sector should solve this problem through the amendment of laws and regulations, new technology, and other forms of support. In addition, it should seek out various solutions and ways to fund these solutions.

The problem is that the authority of the management office is extremely weak in comparison to the burden of its obligations to be fulfilled under the current law. Therefore, even if the law delegates the role of resolving noise problems to the management office, doubt remains as to whether the delegation would be effective considering that the degree of noise can be felt differently by each individual.

6. Safety problems in multi-family housing exposed to natural disasters

On November 15, 2017, a 5.4-magnitude earthquake occurred in the northern part of Buk-gu, Pohang, Gyeongsangbuk-do. The earthquake was the second-strongest since records began through the Korea Meteorological Administration, after the 5.8-magnitude earthquake that rocked Gyeongju in September 2016.

Although the government research team concluded that the earthquake was caused by the injection of water into the ground at a nearby geothermal power plant, doubts and questions have arisen regarding the veracity of this claim.

The earthquake that hit Pohang caused more than 57,000 cases of property damage worth 85 billion won.

The salient problem is that the earthquake exerted significant damage on buildings in the city, including multi-family housing.

In particular, as a large number of residents are clustered together in multi-family housing, measures for minimizing damage should be prepared in case of a disaster or accident, regardless of the right and wrong of the situation. [Figure 4] shows the damage inflicted on a building where the ground floor was constructed with pilotis to replace the parking area and increase the floor area ratio. In this case, it is obvious that the building would collapse if a disaster occurs.

The Earthquake Response Manual provided by the National Disaster and Safety Portal covers only common-sense and basic instructions. The manual should also provide appropriate and detailed information and course of action for communities where large numbers of people reside, for example, multi-family housing, and contain content including prompt guidance by the management office or safety manager. Mandatory earthquake drills should be conducted to familiarize occupants with the recommended course of action.

(Figure 4) Piloti of an apartment building damaged by earthquake in Pohang

Source: Park et al. (2018)

Yoon (2008) emphasizes the need for multi-family housing management offices to implement emergency measures against earthquakes in a study titled "Current Status and Improvement Plan of Measures for Seismic Risk Reduction and Management in Korea." Yoon argues that the central and local governments, and each facility management body should establish an Emergency Action Plan (EAP) that allows a disaster management manager to allocate human and material resources promptly and efficiently to initiate rescue activities.

The importance of periodic drills is evident in the well-known story of the Morgan Stanley Miracle during the 9/11 terror attacks. When the World Trade Center collapsed during the terrorist attacks of September 11, 2001, approximately 3,000 people were killed. However, although Morgan Stanley, a global investment banking company, was located on the 73rd floor, only 13 out of its 2,700 employees died. It is said that because the company had conducted emergency evacuation training four times a year for more than eight years, it was able to save the lives of its employees. Despite opposition from some executives, Rick Rescorla, a security consultant for Morgan Stanley, tenaciously conducted evacuation drills in order to familiarize employees with evacuation procedures. As a result, most employees were able to escape from the 73rd floor of the building, which collapsed within the space of ten minutes.

Natural disasters can occur anywhere on the planet. The expectation that natural disasters will not happen due to geological conditions in the vicinity negatively impacts notions of safety. Since multi-family housing are constantly occupied by many people, it is necessary for more elaborate safety-related plans and systems to be devised and implemented.

There may be opposition from residents, the council of occupants' representatives, and employees of the management company, but those in charge of safety management should make the effort to protect the lives of residents with a mindset to prepare seriously for disasters without hesitation. In addition, the law must be revised to make this practice mandatory.

Natural disasters are absolutely not improbable events isolated to other countries.

References

Kang, E. T. et al. (2018). A Case Study of Unreasonable Interference and Inappropriate Instructions. Korea Research Institute of Housing Management.

Ministry of the Interior and Safety. The Natural Disaster Response Manual. The National Disaster and Safety Portal. Retrieved from http://www.safekorea.go.kr/idsiSFK/neo/main/main.html

Kim, C. U. (2016). The Management Office in a Crisis, People Standing on the Edge of a Cliff. The *Korea Apartment News*. Retrieved from http://www.hapt.co.kr/news/articleView.html?idxno=35441

Park, J. (November 13, 2018). A Security Guards Assaulted for not Wearing a Vest While on Duty. SBS news. Retrieved from http://news.sbs.co.kr/news/endPage.do?news_id=N1005015137

Park, H. G. et al. (2018). A Study on the Preparedness for Earthquake for Earthquake-prone Buildings Including Piloti-type Buildings. Ministry of Land, Infrastructure and Transport.

Yoon, J. B. (2008). Current Status and Improvement Plan of Measures for Seismic Risk Reduction and Management in Korea. The Korean Academy of Science and Technology.

Lee, G. S. (2017). Old Society, Old Infrastructure, Old Apartments. *The Korea Apartment News.* Retrieved from http://www.hapt.co.kr/news/articleView.html?idxno=36795

Lee, J. W. (2015). A Study on the Government's Measures to Support for Solving Problems of Between-floor noise in Multi-Family Housing. (Master's thesis). Ajou University Graduate School of Public Affairs.

Lee, J. H. (2016). (Professor of the Department of Occupational and Environmental Medicine at University of Ulsan College of Medicine). Between-floor noise. Environment and Health Subcommittee of the Korean Medical Association. Retrieved from https://www.doctorsnews.co.kr/news/articleView.html?idxno=108165

Jung, C. H. (2009). A Study on the State of the Between-floor noise in Multi-Family Housing and Improvement Plan. (Master's thesis). Daegu University Graduate School of Industry and Public Administration.

Ha, S. K. et al. (2014). *Contemporary Multifamily Housing Management: Theory and Practice*. Seoul: Parkyoungsa.

CHAPTER 7

Measures to Revitalize Communities in Multi-Family Housing

CHAPTER 7

Measures to Revitalize Communities in Multi-Family Housing

Eun-Taek Kang,
Senior Researcher of the Korea Research Institute of Housing Management

1. Concept and necessity of the revitalization of communities

1) Concept of communities in multi-family housing

In general, a community is defined as a group or organization that shares a sense of belonging based on a certain location (Lee, 2018). Wikipedia defines a community as a social unit that shares a place with the same interests and thoughts. In sum, a community exists on the basis of location and refers to an organization that seeks to promote balanced co-existence, co-prosperity, and co-development within the relationships among the people living at the said location.

Applying the concept of a community to multi-family housing, the community of multi-family housing can be defined as a group consisting of residents living in multi-family housing in a certain geographical area, who aim to achieve common goals or values through mutual exchanges and cooperation.

2) The need for revitalizing communities

Due to the rapid economic growth and the increase in the housing demand, Korea decided to supply multi-family housing as part of the policy to supply housing quickly in a short period of time. Most notably, Korea built the first and second New Towns as a policy measure to supply multi-family housing. The supply of multi-family housing mainly through the construction of new apartments was at the core of New Towns and large-scale housing site development projects.

This policy of supplying multi-family housing was successful in providing housing quickly. However, various issues occurred among multi-family housing occupants due to feelings of disconnection from neighbors, absence of the sense of community, an enclosed housing environment, and lack of mutual understanding as residents of multi-family housing. As a measure to address these issues, an initiative called Make Our Neighborhood a Better Place to Live was launched to revitalize communities in multi-family housing.

Specifically, the background and necessity of revitalizing communities in multi-family housing can be examined in the four following aspects (Lee, 2018). First, social changes and rapid state-led economic growth aggravated imbalances. Since the 2000s, Korean society has suffered a number of social problems such as a low birthrate, aging, deepening inequality and polarization, slowdown of growth, and decreased demand for development, which made it difficult to establish "communality" as the basis of local communities.

Second, there is a growing need for resident participation and community revitalization. As community-building became difficult and a range of social issues arose, it has become important to strive to create places for occupants to lead decent lives. In order to restore and revitalize the community, it is necessary to devise measures to promote human-centric development based on the participation and exchanges of people who reside in a certain "place" as well as the characteristics of the region.

Third, the need for revitalizing communities in multi-family housing as a new form of community has emerged. Multi-family housing is considered to represent the trend of individualization and the disappearance of communal life in the modern world, rather than relationships between people in traditional towns. Therefore, there is a lack of public awareness of the importance of creating multi-family housing communities. Indeed, various problems occur in multi-family housing due to the lack of communication between residents, such as between-floor noise and parking issues.

Lastly, there is not enough support to raise awareness of the need for the revitalization of multi-family housing communities. As more people are becoming interested in the revitalization of communities and participating in such efforts, the central and local governments are presenting various policies and projects to support communities, allocating budgets accordingly and providing required support. However, such assistance is mostly targeted at communities in traditional towns and regions, and there is a lack of awareness and support toward multi-family housing communities as a new model of settlements.

Therefore, it is necessary to identify measures to reinvigorate communities in multi-family housing in order to restore the relationship among residents of multi-family housing and to create a new culture in such communities.

2. Policies and projects related to the multi-family housing community

1) Central government policies and projects

The central government policies and projects related to communities are implemented separately by the various government agencies. The central government focuses on building and vitalizing communities by raising awareness and promoting participation among residents through these policies and projects. The major policies and projects are as follows.

First, the Ministry of the Interior and Safety is promoting the Building the Village of Hope Project. As the ratio of residence in multi-family housing including apartments is increasing across the nation, the Building the Village of Hope Project (public contest under the theme of seniors and apartment communities) aims to establish the multi-family housing community based on communication between occupants and autonomy in addressing issues related to multi-family housing. The Ministry provides subsidies of up to 50 million won to entities that engage in various community activities to realize self-governance within multi-family housing such as social services, resident integration, living conditions improvement, and nursery education activities.

Second, the Ministry of Agriculture, Food and Rural Affairs is carrying out policy projects for the revitalization of communities at the village level. In order to facilitate the vitalization of village communities, the Ministry is promoting various policies and projects, such as the Making a Unique Village Project and the General Agricultural, Mountain and Fishing Villages Development Project. To this end, the Ministry is making various attempts to vitalize resident communities, such as the Agricultural and Fishing Villages Field Forum and the Promotion Committee of Village Consultative Organization. In particular, in order to invigorate communities, the Ministry requires residents to complete multi-phase resident education courses (preparation phase, entry phase, development phase, self-reliance phase), and supports the Resident Capacity-building Project by utilizing separately-allocated budgets.

Third, the Ministry of Land, Infrastructure and Transport is advancing the community revitalization project through the Urban Renewal New Deal Project. As part of efforts to promote the Urban Renewal New Deal Project, the Ministry helps communities of local residents to solve regional problems autonomously through the Urban Renewal University. In particular, the Ministry provides budgets to revitalize the Urban Renewal University so that local residents can complete education courses in four phases, which are designed to help residents to contemplate and address local issues by themselves. In addition, the Ministry also holds a nationwide public competition to fund projects that are generated after

Table 1 Central government's policies and projects for vitalizing the multi-family housing community

Category	Ministry of the Interior and Safety (Building the Village of Hope Project)	Ministry of Agriculture, Food and Rural Affairs (Agricultural, Mountain and Fishing Villages Development Project)	Ministry of Land, Infrastructure and Transport (Urban Renewal New Deal Project)
Summary	Restoring and fostering communities to encourage residents of multi-family housing to solve problems autonomously	Enhancing the quality of life for residents of farming and fishing villages and revitalizing the community by developing rural areas (village)	Strengthening the competitiveness of underdeveloped cities by restoring and revitalizing the communities of residents
Support scope	Multi-family housing	Eup, myeon, villages (region)	Underdeveloped areas within a city
Promoting body	Multi-family housing communities	Promotion committee	Urban renewal residents' council
Supported project	Community service, resident solidarity, living condition improvement, nursery education	Settlement environment, industrial economy, social culture, resident capacity-building	Social integration (regional capacity enhancement, community space creation, residential welfare realization, job creation, city's competitiveness restoration)
Funding amount	Within 50 million won	Within 500 million won for each village unit and within 30 million won for a field forum	Within 30 million won for the Urban Renewal University
Selection method	Open call	Open call	Open call
Resident capacity building phase	First round education, second round education	Preparation phase, entry phase, development phase, and self-reliance phase	Initial proliferation stage (four-stage education course)- Project promotion stage
Support period	One to two years	Within one year for the Residents' Capacity Building Project, and three to five years for the Village Project	Three to five years for urban areas

Source: Lee (2018).

finishing the education course for helping residents to identify and resolve urban problems autonomously.

2) Local government policies and projects

All local governments carry out projects to revitalize communities of multi-family housing. The representative cases of Seoul and Gyeonggi-do are as follows.

The Seoul Metropolitan Government (SMG) enacted and operates the Municipal Ordinance on Support for Village Community Building in order to create a city where citizens participate and feel satisfied. Separately, the city enacted and is implementing the Municipal Ordinance on Support for Community Housing Vitalization. In accordance with the ordinances, it established and operates the Comprehensive Community Support Center to support communities, and devised and implements Basic Plans to Foster Village Communities. The city divides the formation stage of village communities into three stages (seed stage, sprout stage, and hope stage) and provides tailored support.

Table 2 Details of support from the SMG for building a village community at each formation stage

Stage	Target	Contents of support
Seed stage	Villages with a weak community	Revitalizing residents' gatherings, developing village projects, fostering and appointing village leaders, educating and training village workers
Sprout stage	Villages with the foundation of a community	Consulting, materializing developed projects through support for planning, educating residents, educating and training village workers, forming village activity support groups and providing related supports
Hope stage	Villages with active community activities	Implementing various village projects for childcare, culture, economy and environment, providing education to residents, and supporting new projects development for securing sustainability

Source: Seoul Institute (2014).

The Gyeonggi Provincial Government encourages residents to develop and propose voluntary and creative projects, and supports the projects through evaluation based on the Municipal Ordinance on Support for Building Warm and Happy Communities in Gyeonggi-do. The province installed and operates the Village Building Committee with the aim to develop and assist projects in conjunction and cooperation between departments based on the Converged Village Building Promotion Plan. Furthermore, the Gyeonggi Provincial Government has a system where residents propose their own projects, which are selected through evaluation and promoted on an ongoing basis. It also carries out projects for resident welfare, job creation, healthcare, education, and childcare.

The Suwon City Government is implementing the Village Renaissance Project based on the Municipal Ordinance for Village Building. The city established the promotion strategy in stages: the first stage is for building a regional village renaissance; the second stage is for building a Suwon-style village renaissance; and the third stage is for building a Korean-style village renaissance. Suwon carries out projects where residents can solve problems autonomously through regular and ad hoc contests, and aims to induce greater participation by residents and draw their attention by developing such contests into regional events.

3. Vitalization of communities at the resident level

Every occupant of multi-family housing is a main actor in vitalizing the community in multi-family housing. Above all, however, it is necessary to find a leader who is essential for leading a community with a sense of duty, and establish an organization under the leader to continuously develop and implement programs that will garner a positive response from residents.

The revitalization of the community in multi-family housing at the resident level can be achieved according to the following stages: Finding the seeds of a community → Understanding our complex → Developing community programs together → Encouraging participation and blossoming → Sustaining the fruits of our efforts. The key details of each stage are as follows.

Figure 1 Community activity with apartment resident

Source: The Korea Apartment News (2018.12.05)

Figure 2 The process of community revitalization by residents

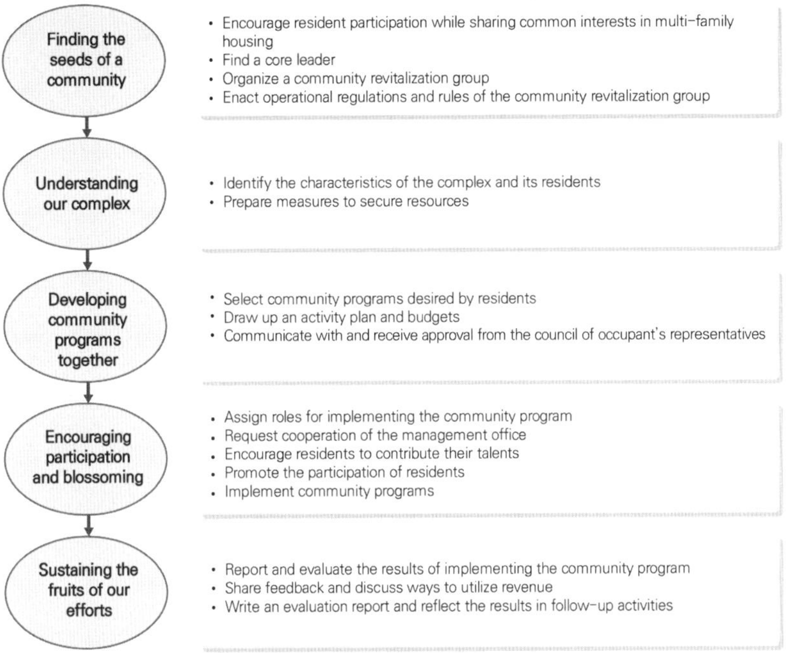

Source: Ministry of Land, Infrastructure and Transport (2017).

References

Ministry of Land, Infrastructure and Transport. (2017). The Program Operation Manual for Apartment Community Vitalization.

Seoul Institute. (2014). Master Plan for Seoul Village Community (proposal).

Lee, S. J. (2018). A Study on Measures for Vitalizing Communities in Multi-Family Housing. ChungNam Institute.

CHAPTER 8

Direction of Development in Multi-Family Housing Management

CHAPTER 8

Direction of Development in Multi-Family Housing Management

Byung-Nam Park,
Secretary General of the Korea Housing Managers Association

1. Development history of the management system

Multi-family housing has taken root as the most important housing type in Korea. Multi-family housing accounts for more than 75% of all house types, and has become an important asset at the national level. Therefore, the management of multi-family housing has become one of the most important national affairs, and matters concerning the management of multi-family housing are stipulated in the Multi-Family Housing Management Act.

The multi-family housing management system began with national-level focus in the early 1980s. The 40-year history of the multi-family housing management system can be classified into three phases: Management System Phase 1 where the management of multi-family housing was conducted pursuant to the Decree on Multi-Family Housing Management under the Housing Construction Promotion Act; Management System Phase 2 where the management system became settled with the enactment of the Housing Act on May 29, 2003; and Management System Phase 3 where management began to be conducted by specialists with the enactment of the Multi-Family Housing Management Act on August 12, 2015.

2. The multi-family housing management system

During Management System Phase 1, efforts were made to establish the roles and functions of entities involved in multi-family housing management, including the government, occupants, and housing managers. In addition, the subject of management was divided into two categories: multi-family housing subject to compulsory management and multi-family housing not subject to compulsory management, thereby establishing a dual system. This phase can be considered to be an early stage where the foundation of multi-family housing management was laid by establishing standards for levying management expenses, standard management rules, and regulations to ensure the rights of occupants.

In Management System Phase 2, the management expenses disclosure system called K-apt was established with the aim of upholding the public's right to know about the imposition, collection, and operation of management expenses. As part of efforts to strengthen the expertise and efficiency in the management of multi-family housing, various related laws were revised to settle the management system. In order to enhance the transparency of management, Guidelines for Selecting Project Operator was devised and implemented, including instructions for the selection of a housing management service provider. In addition, an institutional strategy pursued the establishment of community culture in multi-family housing. The Defect Examination and Dispute Mediation Committee was established to protect citizens' rights and interests, and the Multi-Family Housing Management Support Center to provide public services and establish the public support system. The management system was stabilized during this phase.

In Management System Phase 3, the management system was improved in a direction to promote occupants' participation and raise awareness of management affairs while enhancing the quality of management services provided by management employees, thereby satisfying the public need for management. Institutional efforts were also made to increase the efficiency of multi-family housing management, including the preparation of related regulations, management manuals tailored to the specialized management era, the quality evaluation system and the provision on the indication of the performance rating of multi-family housing.

The Multi-Family Housing Management Dispute Mediation Committee was established to implement the policy of securing a safety net for the daily lives of occupants, and to address various disputes related to between-floor noise, smoking, pets, and others. In Management System Phase 3, the public support system established during Phase 2 began in earnest, and local governments' supervision was tightened, for example, by conducting investigations on management status through active government intervention in multi-family housing management affairs.

3. Development direction of the multi-family housing management system

Korea's multi-family housing management system has a 40-year history. The government had previously focused on housing supply policies that increase the supply of multi-family housing. Consequently, policies related to multi-family housing management were often overlooked. As a result, many problems have begun to occur in the multi-family housing management system. In particular, as high-rise buildings were constructed on a large scale and large numbers of occupants could reside in multi-family housing complexes, the problems of the multi-family housing management system were brought to the surface. This is a situation that requires urgent reforms.

Previously, Chapter 2 examined the challenges facing multi-family housing management. In sum, the challenges included: 1. a lack of consumer-oriented management services; 2. management focused on physical components; 3. an increase in the demand for socio-economic management due to socio-demographical changes; 4. an absence of awareness about horizontal relationships between decision-making bodies and enforcement bodies for management; and 5. employment instability among housing managers and the absence of a performance evaluation system.[1]

The development direction of the management system can be presented with a focus on the resolution of these challenges. First, management services should be provided in consideration of the safety and convenience of occupants. The scope of management services should be expanded to establish a safety net for occupants' daily lives including between-floor noise, energy efficiency, smoking on the premises, fire, and disaster and safety management. However, the expansion of the service scope could result in a lack of manpower and an increase in expenses. Therefore, in order to provide high-quality residential services, it is necessary to assign more housing management specialists and consider measures to supplement expenses. To expand the assignment of specialists, for example, on the basis of 1,000 households, one qualified specialist can be dispatched additionally for every 1,000 households. Currently, one housing manager is assigned to each multi-family housing regardless of the number of households in the complex, because the criteria for the assignment of housing managers remain the same as when they were first introduced.

Second, it is necessary to draw public attention to the management of multi-family housing. Currently, with regard to the roles and functions of each actor involved in the multi-family housing management such as the government, occupants, and management specialists, Korea is unable to achieve balance in their independent roles. Consequently, the level of interest and participation among occupants is low, and thus it has been difficult to establish a management culture and communities in multi-family housing. In addition, in areas where the government's role is limited, specialists and occupants should assume such roles and functions to

1 Refer to 3. Urgent issues of multi-family housing in Chapter 2. Significance of Multi-Family Housing Management.

further develop the relevant system, but that is not the case in reality. It is necessary to create a management culture by promoting participation in the management process through the comprehensive examination and adjustment of roles and functions of each actor.

Third, there is a need to develop housing management services that consider changes in the demographic structure including low fertility, aging population, and an increase in the number of single households. These services could include a co-parenting support system and the assignment of social workers to provide everyday convenience services for the elderly. However, as this also entails problems concerning a lack of specialists and increased costs, the aforementioned issues of a lack of manpower and an increase in expenses should be addressed simultaneously. In preparation for the population decrease, buildings should be managed to prolong their lifespans. To do so, there is a need to resolve problems related to the long-term repair plan. Under the current system of multi-family housing management, both occupants and management specialists face difficulties in performing long-term repair work according to the long-term repair plan. Management specialists have to diagnose facilities according to the long-term repair plan and conduct repair work in accordance with the diagnosis result. However, they face problems such as the inadequacy of the long-term repair plan, reserves for long-term repairs, and repair work plan. On the other hand, occupants lack the expertise in selecting a suitable company that can implement a long-term repair plan and calculating the expenses required for repair work. It is necessary to coordinate the items in the long-term repair plan with the actual conditions and properly maintain the input system for long-term repair work. In addition, the management of buildings in a multi-family housing complex should be performed in accordance with their lifecycle by maintaining records on repair work under the long-term repair plan.

Fourth, trust is required in multi-family housing management. One of the major issues in Korea's multi-family housing management system is the management expenses. As multi-family housing has been supplied in the form of high-rise buildings constructed on a large scale, the scale of the total management expenses of each complex has expanded significantly. Disputes among occupants concerning management expenses have also increased. Occupants file complaints against various operational problems from levying and collecting management expenses to the usage of the expenses. Therefore, it is necessary to dedicate institutional efforts to ensure efficiency, transparency, equity, fairness, expertise, and credibility with regard to the management expenses of multi-family housing.

Fifth, there are problems regarding the small scale and roles of business entities specializing in management services for multi-family housing. Currently, Korea is unable to guarantee the quality of management due to the small scale and insufficient expertise of multi-family housing management companies. In particular, entrusted management companies are operated solely on an entrustment commission basis rather than by concluding a subcontract due to their poor financing, and thus are not operated under a stable profit system. As entrusted management companies fail to generate sufficient profits, they are unable to support overall management affairs, such as technical support for on-site management affairs and prevention of various risks. In addition, there have been frequent disputes over the boundaries of management duties as clear boundaries have not been established with regard to such duties by the council of occupants' representatives under the entrusted management contract. Therefore, it is necessary to enhance the ability to support management affairs through the sound development of housing management services.

4. Conclusion

Korea's multi-family housing management system was established to solve the management problems that occur when housing is supplied on a large scale. Since then, the management system developed to reflect opinions of residents and experts. Since the housing management system was first introduced in Korea, housing managers as management experts and the Korea Housing Managers Association as the competent organization have made efforts to improve and develop the management system. Currently, as Korea's multi-family housing management system evolved, the system has become established and reinforced as a public management system.

Therefore, Korea's management services for multi-family housing are increasingly becoming recognized as public services. The aim of public services should be to ensure the residential stability of the people. The current form of the public management system gives prominence to the supervision of management, rather than providing public services. Multi-family housing could require supervision by a public organization as a national asset. However, there is a concern that, if the state focuses only on supervision, the occupants of multi-family housing will be forced to live in an uncomfortable atmosphere, or an innocent citizen may be wrongfully branded as a law-breaker. Therefore, in order to further develop the public management system, adequate support should be provided for occupants to autonomously conduct the reasonable and efficient management of multi-family housing, with an emphasis on stabilizing housing for the public.

References

Bang, K. S. (2013). *Theory of Multi-Family Housing Management.* Seoul: Buyonsa.

Ha, S. K., Kim, J. I., Jun, M. J. & Moon, T. H. (2007). *How to Make Cities Sustainable*. Seoul: Boseonggak.

Ha, S. K. et al. (2014). *A New Paradigm for Multifamily Housing Management,* Seoul: Parkyoungsa.

APPENDIX

MULTI-FAMILY HOUSING MANAGEMENT ACT

APPENDIX

MULTI-FAMILY HOUSING MANAGEMENT ACT[1]

Act No. 13474, Aug. 11, 2015
Amended by Act No. 13499, Aug. 28, 2015
Act No. 13508, Sep. 1, 2015
Act No. 13676, Dec. 29, 2015
Act No. 13687, Dec. 29, 2015
Act No. 13786, Jan. 19, 2016
Act No. 13805, Jan. 19, 2016
Act No. 14093, Mar. 22, 2016
Act No. 14709, Mar. 21, 2017
Act No. 14793, Apr. 18, 2017

Article 1 (Purpose)

The purpose of this Act is to contribute to improving residential standards for the people by helping them manage multi-family housing transparently, safely, and efficiently by prescribing matters concerning the management of multi-family housing.

Article 2 (Definitions)

(1) The definitions of terms used in this Act shall be as follows: *<Amended by Act No. 13499, Aug. 28, 2015; Act No. 13676, Dec. 29, 2015; Act No. 13805, Jan. 19, 2016; Act No. 14793, Apr. 18, 2017>*

1. The term "multi-family housing" means the following housing and facilities. In such cases, welfare facilities sold to the general public shall be excluded:
   (a) Multi-family housing under subparagraph 3 of Article 2 of the Housing Act;
   (b) A building which consists of facilities other than housing and housing built compositely in the same building after obtaining a building permit under Article 11 of the Building Act;
   (c) Auxiliary facilities under subparagraph 13 of Article 2 of the Housing Act and welfare facilities under subparagraph 14 of the aforesaid Article.
2. The term "multi-family housing subject to compulsory management" means multi-family housing upon which specific obligations are imposed, such as multi-family housing which must have a person who manages the relevant multi-family housing professionally and organize an autonomous decision-making body compulsorily, among multi-family housing with at least 150 households, and the range of multi-family housing subject to compulsory management shall be

1 Source: Korea Law Translation Center.

prescribed by Presidential Decree;

3. The term "multi-family housing complex" means a housing complex under subparagraph 12 of Article 2 of the Housing Act;
4. The term "mixed housing complex" means a multi-family housing complex in which multi-family housing for the purpose of sale and rental housing are built compositely;
5. The term "occupant" means an owner of multi-family housing, his/her spouse representing such owner and lineal ascendants and descendants;
6. The term "user" means a person, etc. who leases and uses multi-family housing (excluding a lessee of rental housing);
7. The term "occupant, etc." means an occupant and a user;
8. The term "council of occupants' representatives" means an autonomous decision-making body organized pursuant to Article 14 to decide important matters concerning management on behalf of occupants, etc. of multi-family housing;
9. The term "management rules" means rules of autonomy prescribed by occupants, etc. pursuant to Article 18 (2) to protect occupants, etc. of multi-family housing and to maintain orderly residential life;
10. The term "management entity" means the following persons managing multi-family housing:
    (a) The head of the management office of multi-family housing, who represents an autonomous management body under Article 6 (1);
    (b) A business entity before it transfers managerial affairs pursuant to Article 13 (1);
    (c) A housing management service provider;
    (d) A rental business operator;
    (e) A housing rental management business operator (limited to where he/she conducts affairs concerning the maintenance, repair and improvement of facilities, and housing management) under subparagraph 11 of Article 2 of the Special Act on Private Rental Housing;
11. The term "probationary housing manager" means a person issued a certificate upon passing an examination for probationary housing managers pursuant to Article 67 (1);
12. The term "housing manager" means a person issued a certificate of qualification as housing manager pursuant to Article 67 (2);
13. The term "housing manager, etc." means a probationary housing manager and housing manager;
14. The term "housing management services" means a service that manages multi-family housing subject to compulsory management after being entrusted with the management thereof by occupants, etc. to manage multi-family housing in a safe and efficient manner;
15. The term "housing management service provider" means a person who provides housing management services, registered pursuant to Article 52 (1);
16. and 17. Deleted. *<by Act No. 13805, Jan. 19, 2016>*
18. The term "long-term repair plan" means a long-term plan formulated pursuant to Article 29 (1) concerning the replacement, repair, etc. of major facilities necessary to use multi-family housing safely and efficiently long-term;
19. The term "rental housing" means private rental housing under the Special Act on Private Rental Housing and public rental housing under the Special Act on Public Housing;
20. The term "rental business operator" means a rental business operator under subparagraph 7 of Article 2 of the Special Act on Private Rental Housing and a public housing business operator under Article 4 (1) of the Special Act on Public Housing;
21. The term "council of lessees' representatives" means a council of representatives of lessees under Article 52 of the Special Act on Private Rental Housing and a council of lessees' representatives applied mutatis mutandis pursuant to Article 50 of the Special Act on Public Housing.

(2) The Housing Act shall apply to the definitions of terms not otherwise expressly prescribed by this Act.

Article 3 (Obligations of State, etc.)

(1) Where the State and local governments formulate and implement policy concerning the management of multi-family housing, they shall endeavor for the following:

1. They shall endeavor so that occupants, etc. who reside in multi-family housing may live a comfortable and liveable residential life;
2. They shall endeavor so that multi-family housing may be managed in a transparent, systematic and peaceful manner;
3. They shall endeavor so that industries related to the management of multi-family housing may seek sound development.

(2) The management entity shall manage multi-family housing in an efficient and safe manner.

(3) Occupants, etc. shall show consideration for neighbors and provide cooperation in affairs of the management entity so that order of community life may be maintained.

Article 4 (Relationship to Other Acts)

(1) The Housing Act shall apply to matters not otherwise expressly prescribed by this Act concerning the management of multi-family housing.

(2) This Act shall apply matters not otherwise expressly prescribed by the Special Act on Private Rental Housing or the Special Act on Public Housing concerning the management of rental housing. *<Amended by Act No. 13499, Aug. 28, 2015>*

Article 5 (Methods of Management of Multi - Family Housing)

(1) Occupants, etc. shall conduct autonomous management of multi-family housing subject to compulsory management pursuant to Article 6 (1) or entrust the management of such multi-family housing to a housing management service provider pursuant to Article 7 (1).

(2) Where occupants, etc. prescribe or alter the method of management of multi-family housing, they shall do so as prescribed by Presidential Decree.

Article 6 (Autonomous Management)

(1) Where occupants, etc. of multi-family housing subject to compulsory management decide to conduct autonomous management of multi-family housing, the council of occupants' representatives shall appoint the head of the management office of multi-family housing as the representative of an autonomous management body and organize the autonomous management body which has technical human resources and equipment prescribed by Presidential Decree.

(2) Where occupants, etc. of multi-family housing subject to compulsory management alters the method of management of such multi-family housing to autonomous management from the management thereof entrusted to a housing management service provider, the council of occupants' representatives shall organize an autonomous management body under paragraph (1) by no later than the expiration date of such entrusted management.

Article 7 (Management Entrusted)

(1) Where occupants, etc. of multi-family housing subject to compulsory management decide to entrust the management of multi-family housing to a housing management service provider, the council of occupants' representatives shall select the housing management service provider in accordance with the following guidelines:

1. The council of occupants' representatives shall select the housing management service provider through an information processing system (hereinafter referred to as "method of electronic bidding") under subparagraph 2 of Article 2 of the Framework Act on Electronic Documents and Transactions: Provided, That where a method of selection, etc. is prescribed and announced by the Minister of Land, Infrastructure and Transport, in which case it is difficult to use electronic bidding, the council of occupants' representatives may opt not to select the housing management service provider through electronic bidding;
2. The council of occupants' representatives shall follow methods prescribed by Presidential Decree, such as other methods of bidding.

(2) Where occupants, etc. are not satisfied with management services provided by the

existing housing management service provider, they may request the council of occupants' representatives to restrict the participation of the existing housing management service provider in the bidding for the selection of a new housing management service provider, as prescribed by Presidential Decree. In such cases, the council of occupants' representatives shall comply with such request.

Article 8 (Joint Management and Separate Management)

(1) Where the council of occupants' representatives deems it necessary for the management of the relevant multi-family housing, it may require a housing management service provider to jointly manage adjacent multi-family housing (including a rental housing complex) or to separately manage multi-family housing by dividing the relevant multi-family housing into a unit of at least 500 households, as prescribed by Ordinance of the Ministry of Land, Infrastructure and Transport.

(2) Joint management under paragraph (1) shall be applicable only to cases meeting the standards prescribed by Ordinance of the Ministry of Land, Infrastructure and Transport, in which case written consent of a majority of occupants, etc. is obtained for each complex (in cases of a rental housing complex, referring to where written consent of the rental business operator and the council of lessees' representatives is obtained).

Article 9 (Management Body of Multi-Family Housing)

(1) The council of occupants' representatives or the management entity shall organize a management body of multi-family housing (including an autonomous management body under Article 6 (1)) for the maintenance, repair, management, etc., of the common areas of multi-family housing.

(2) Necessary matters concerning the composition, function, operation, etc. of a management body of multi-family housing shall be prescribed by Presidential Decree.

Article 10 (Management of Mixed Housing Complex)

(1) The council of occupants' representatives and the rental business operator shall jointly determine matters concerning the management of a mixed housing complex. In such cases, in the mixed housing complex where the council of lessees' representatives has been organized, the rental business operator shall consult with the council of lessees' representatives on matters under the subparagraphs of Article 52 (3) of the Special Act on Private Rental Housing. *<Amended by Act No. 13499, Aug. 28, 2015>*

(2) Matters concerning management to be jointly determined under paragraph (1) and necessary matters concerning methods, procedures, etc. for making joint determinations shall be prescribed by Presidential Decree.

Article 11 (Transfer of Management)

(1) The business entity who has built multi-family housing subject to compulsory management shall manage such multi-family housing until a majority of prospective occupants moves into multi-family housing, and where a majority of prospective occupants has moved into multi-family housing, the business entity shall notify occupants, etc. of the fact and request them to manage the relevant multi-family housing, as prescribed by Presidential Decree.

(2) Upon receipt of a request under paragraph (1), occupants shall organize the council of occupants' representatives whose members are occupants within three months from the date they receive such request.

(3) Where occupants, etc. determine the method of management of the relevant multi-family housing (where they select the method of entrusted management, including the selection of a housing management service provider), the chairperson of the council of occupants' representatives (where a person performs duties on behalf of the chairperson, including the person who performs duties on behalf of the chairperson; hereinafter the same shall apply) shall notify the business entity of the method of management thereof, and report such method of management thereof to the competent Special Self-Governing City Mayor, the competent Special Self-Governing Province Governor, or the head of the competent Si/Gun/Gu (referring to the head of an autonomous Gu; hereinafter the same shall apply;

hereinafter the Special Self-Governing City Mayor, the Special Self-Governing Province Governor, or the head of a Si/Gun/Gu shall be referred to as "head of a Si/Gun/Gu"), as prescribed by Presidential Decree. The foregoing shall also apply where any matters reported are altered.

Article 12 (Selection of Housing Management Service Provider by Business Entity)

Where the council of occupants' representatives fails to give notification under Article 11 (3) or to organize an autonomous management body under Article 6 (1), the business entity shall select a housing management service provider. In such cases, the business entity shall notify the council of occupants' representatives and the head of the competent Si/Gun/Gu of such fact.

Article 13 (Transfer of Managerial Affairs)

(1) In any of the following cases, the business entity shall transfer managerial affairs of multi-family housing to the relevant management entity, as prescribed by Presidential Decree:

1. Where the business entity receives notification of the selection of a housing management service provider from the chairperson of the council of occupants' representatives pursuant to Article 11 (3);
2. Where an autonomous management body is organized pursuant to Article 6 (1);
3. Where a housing management service provider is selected pursuant to Article 12.

(2) Where the management entity of multi-family housing is replaced, the existing management entity shall transfer managerial affairs of the relevant multi-family housing to a new management entity by applying paragraph (1) mutatis mutandis.

Article 14 (Composition, etc. of Council of Occupants' Representatives)

(1) The council of occupants' representatives shall be comprised of at least four persons, who are representatives elected according to electoral districts prescribed by the management rules in proportion to the number of households in each building (hereinafter referred to as "representative of each building"). In such cases, an electoral district may be established by combining two or more buildings or dividing a building by corridors or floors.

(2) Where one multi-family housing complex is divided into several sections and built one by one (in cases of rental housing, referring to where it is converted to housing for sale), occupants, etc. of a section of multi-family housing who move into such multi-family housing first may organize the council of occupants' representatives pursuant to paragraph (1): Provided, That where a majority of prospective occupants of the next section moves into multi-family housing, a further new council of occupants' representatives shall be organized again.

(3) A representative of each building shall be elected through universal suffrage, equal suffrage, by direction election and secret ballot of occupants, etc. of an electoral district among occupants (where an occupant is a corporation, referring to the representative thereof) meeting the following requirements as at the deadline for submitting various documents (hereafter in this Article, referred to as "deadline for submitting documents") prescribed in the public notice of the election of the representative of each building, as prescribed by Presidential Decree:

1. Occupants shall have continuously resided for a period exceeding that prescribed by Presidential Decree after having obtained resident registration in the relevant multi-family housing complex (excluding where the representative of each building is elected to organize the first council of occupants' representatives or the council of occupants' representatives under the proviso to paragraph (2));
2. Occupants shall have resided in the relevant electoral district after having obtained resident registration.

(4) No person who falls under any of the following as at the deadline for submitting documents shall become the representative of each building, and he/she shall become disqualified accordingly: *<Amended by Act No. 13499, Aug. 28, 2015>*

1. A minor, an adult placed under the protection of a legal guardian or a quasi-incompetent placed under the protection of a legal guardian;
2. A person declared bankrupt who is yet unreinstated;
3. A person in whose case two years have not passed since his/her imprisonment

without labor or heavier punishment was completely executed (including where the execution thereof is deemed completed) or discharged as declared by a court for a crime violating this Act, the Housing Act, the Special Act on Private Rental Housing, the Special Act on Public Housing, the Building Act or the Act on Ownership and Management of Condominium Buildings;

4. A person who is subject to a suspended sentence of the imprisonment without labor or heavier punishment as declared by a court;
5. Other persons prescribed by Presidential Decree.

(5) The council of occupants' representatives shall have the chairperson, the auditor and directors as its executives, as prescribed by Presidential Decree.

(6) Where the council of occupants' representatives holds its meeting, it shall prepare minutes and require the management entity to keep the minutes; where occupants, etc. request the management entity to make the minutes available for perusal or to reproduce the minutes at his/her own expenses, the management entity shall comply with such request, as prescribed by the management rules.

(7) Matters concerning the term of office of representatives of each building or restrictions on the term of office, necessary matters for composing and operating the council of occupants' representatives, such as methods of election and dismissal of representatives of each building or executives of the council of occupants' representatives, and methods of decision-making of the council of occupants' representatives shall be prescribed by Presidential Decree.

(8) Matters to be determined by the council of occupants' representatives shall be the management rules, management expenses, matters concerning the operation of facilities, etc., and the specific details thereof shall be prescribed by Presidential Decree.

Article 15 (Election Management of Representatives, etc. of Each Building)

(1) Occupants, etc. shall organize an election committee (hereinafter referred to as "election committee") to elect or dismiss representatives of each building or executive officers of the council of occupants' representatives.

(2) No person who falls under any of the following shall become members of an election committee, and such person shall become disqualified accordingly:

1. Representatives of each building or candidates for such representatives;
2. The spouse or lineal ascendants or descendants of a person who falls under subparagraph 1;
3. Other persons prescribed by Presidential Decree.

(3) Matters necessary for composing and operating an election committee, such as the number of members of the election committee, methods of electing the chairperson thereof, and methods of decision-making, shall be prescribed by Presidential Decree.

(4) An election committee may request a Gu/Si/Gun election committee having jurisdiction over the relevant location to provide electoral support, such as vote and ballot-counting management, pursuant to Article 2 (1) 3 of the Election Commission Act for the election management under paragraph (1).

Article 16 (Inquiry about Criminal Records of Candidates for Representatives of Each Building)

(1) The chairperson of the election committee (where the election committee has not been organized or the office of the chairperson thereof has become vacant upon his/her resignation, dismissal, etc., referring to the chairperson of the council of occupants' representatives, and where the office of the chairperson of the council of occupants' representatives has also become vacant, referring to the head of the management office) shall conduct criminal background checks of candidates for representatives of each building with the head of a related agency with their consent to verify whether they constitute grounds for disqualification as representatives of a building under the subparagraphs of Article 14 (4).

(2) Necessary matters concerning procedures, methods, etc. for conducting criminal background checks under paragraph (1) shall be prescribed by Presidential Decree.

Article 17 (Education of Members of Council of Occupants' Representatives)

(1) The head of a Si/Gun/Gu shall provide necessary education related to the operation

of the council of occupants' representatives and ethics education for members of the council of occupants' representatives. In such cases, members of the council of occupants' representatives shall complete such education conscientiously.

(2) Education content under paragraph (1) shall include the following:

1. Matters concerning standing rules for the related statutes and the management rules concerning the management of multi-family housing;
2. Matters concerning duties, knowledge, and ethics of members of the council of occupants' representatives;
3. Matters concerning the revitalization of the community of a multi-family housing complex;
4. Matters concerning management expenses, user fees and reserves for long-term repairs;
5. Matters concerning the mediation of disputes between occupants;
6. Matters concerning repairs of defects;
7. Other matters necessary for the operation of the council of occupants' representatives.

(3) Necessary matters concerning the timing and methods of education under paragraph (1), and apportioning expenses therefor, etc. shall be prescribed by Presidential Decree.

Article 18 (Management Rules)

(1) The Special Metropolitan City Mayor, the Metropolitan City Mayor, the Special Self-Governing City Mayor, the Do Governor or the Special Self-Governing Province Governor (hereinafter referred to as "Mayor/Do Governor") shall establish the standing rules for the management rules which serve as criteria for the management or use of multi-family housing to protect occupants, etc. of multi-family housing and to maintain orderly residential life, as prescribed by Presidential Decree.

(2) Occupants, etc. shall establish the management rules by referring to the standing rules for the management rules under paragraph (1). In such cases, matters concerning a rent, etc. of a day care center established in multi-family housing pursuant to Article 21 of the Housing Act shall be determined in consideration of the standing rules for the management rules, the stable operation of a day care center, the improvement of standards for child care services, etc. under paragraph (1). *<Amended by Act No. 13786, Jan. 19, 2016>*

(3) Necessary matters concerning methods, etc. by which occupants, etc. enact or amend the management rules shall be prescribed by Presidential Decree. *<Newly Inserted by Act No. 13786, Jan. 19, 2016>*

(4) Management rules shall also have an effect on those who succeed to the position of occupants, etc. *<Amended by Act No. 13786, Jan. 19, 2016>*

Article 19 (Reporting of Management Rules, etc.)

The chairperson of the council of occupants' representatives (in cases of the enactment of the management rules, referring to the business entity) shall report the following to the head of a Si/Gun/Gu, as prescribed by Presidential Decree. The foregoing shall also apply where reported matters are altered:

1. Enactment or amendment of the management rules;
2. Organization or alteration of the council of occupants' representatives;
3. Other necessary matters prescribed by Presidential Decree.

Article 20 (Prevention, etc. of Noise from Human Activities in Upper Living Spaces)

(1) Occupants, etc. of multi-family housing shall endeavor not to cause harm to other occupants, etc. due to noise from human activities in upper living spaces (including noise between neighboring households; hereinafter referred to as "noise from human activities in upper living spaces"), such as noise which occurs from running or walking motion in multi-family housing.

(2) Occupants, etc. who get harmed due to noise from human activities in upper living spaces under paragraph (1) may notify the management entity of the occurrence of noise from human activities in upper living spaces, and request the management entity to recommend the relevant occupants, etc. who cause noise from human

activities in upper living spaces to cease causing such noise or to take measures for noise abatement. In such cases, the management entity may conduct necessary examinations, such as verification within households, to verify the facts.

(3) Occupants, etc. who cause noise from human activities in upper living spaces shall provide cooperation, such as stopping harm caused by noise from human activities in upper living spaces, in accordance with measures taken and recommendations made by the management entity under paragraph (2).

(4) Notwithstanding measures taken by the management entity under paragraph (2), where noise from human activities in upper living spaces continuously occurs, occupants, etc. who get disturbed by such noise may file an application for mediation with the multi-family housing management dispute mediation committee under Article 71 or the environmental dispute mediation committee under Article 4 of the Environmental Dispute Mediation Act.

(5) The range and standards of noise from human activities in upper living spaces shall be prescribed by Joint Ordinance of the Ministry of Land, Infrastructure and Transport and the Ministry of Environment.

(6) Where necessary, the management entity may provide education for the prevention of noise from human activities in upper living spaces, mediation of disputes, etc. intended for occupants, etc.

(7) Where necessary, occupants, etc. may organize and operate an autonomous organization for the prevention, mediation, education, etc. of disputes due to noise from human activities in upper living spaces.

Article 21 (Revitalization of Community Life)

(1) Occupants, etc. of multi-family housing may autonomously conduct activities necessary for promoting understanding and harmony between occupants, etc., and may organize and operate an organization necessary for the promotion thereof.

(2) The council of occupants' representatives or the management entity may partially subsidize expenses incurred in revitalizing community life from income generated incidentally from the management of multi-family housing, such as proceeds from the sale of recyclables.

(3) Subsidization of expenses under paragraph (2) shall be prescribed by the management rules or determined through a resolution of the council of occupants' representatives to the extent not violating the management rules.

Article 22 (Decision - Making through Electronic Methods)

In any of the following cases, occupants, etc. may make decisions through an electronic method (referring to the method using an information processing system under subparag raph 2 of Article 2 of the Framework Act on Electronic Documents and Transactions or using other information and communications technology), as prescribed by Presidential Decree:

1. Where they elect representatives of each building or executive officers of the council of occupants' representatives;
2. Where they determine or alter the method of managing multi-family housing;
3. Where they enact or amend the management rules;
4. Where they make decisions with written consent, such as cases of determining joint management and separate management pursuant to Article 8;
5. Where they make other decisions in relation to the management of multi-family housing.

Article 23 (Payment, Disclosure, etc. of Management Expenses, etc.)

(1) Occupants, etc. of multi-family housing subject to compulsory management shall pay management expenses necessary for the maintenance and management of such multi-family housing to the management entity.

(2) Necessary matters concerning the details, etc. of management expenses under paragraph (1) shall be prescribed Presidential Decree.

(3) The management entity under paragraph (1) may pay user fees, etc. prescribed by Presidential Decree, which are supposed to be paid by occupants, etc., to a person who is to receive such user fees, etc. on behalf of occupants, etc.

(4) The management entity under paragraph (1) may disclose the following details

(referring to the calculated details of each item, but excluding the details of management expenses imposed on each household) on the Internet homepage of the relevant multi-family housing *[where it has no Internet homepage, referring to a website (limited to where the management entity manages or controls it) provided from an internet portal, whose functions are similar to those of the Internet homepage, the management office of the relevant multi-family housing, its bulletin board, etc.; hereinafter the same shall apply] and the multi-family housing management information system (hereinafter referred to as "multi-family housing management information system") established and operated by the Minister of Land, Infrastructure and Transport pursuant to Article 88 (1), as prescribed by Presidential Decree: Provided, That where it is difficult to disclose the details thereof in the multi-family housing management information system, which are prescribed by Presidential Decree, the management entity may disclose such cases on the Internet homepage of the relevant multi-family housing only:*

1. Management expenses under paragraph (2);
2. User fees, etc. under paragraph (3);
3. Reserves for long-term repairs under Article 30 (1) and the amount accumulated;
4. Other matters prescribed by Presidential Decree.

Article 24 (Deposit for Management Expense)

(1) The management entity may collect expenses incurred in managing and operating the common areas of the relevant multi-family housing (hereinafter referred to as "deposit for management expense") from the owners of multi-family housing.

(2) Where an owner of multi-family housing relinquished his/her ownership, the management entity shall return management expenses on deposit it has collected pursuant to paragraph (1) to such owner: Provided, That where the owner has failed to pay management expenses, user fees, reserves for long-term repairs, etc., the management entity may return the remainder after it settles the amount in arrears from the deposit for management expenses.

(3) Necessary matters concerning collecting, managing, operating, etc. deposit for management expenses shall be prescribed by Presidential Decree.

Article 25 (Selection of Business Operator for Disbursement of Management Expenses, etc.)

Where the management entity of multi-family housing subject to compulsory manage-ment or the council of occupants' representatives thereof intends to select a business operator for the disbursement of money falling under any of Article 23 (4) 1 through 3, a security deposit for repairing defects under Article 38 (1) and money from all the proceeds generated from the relevant multi-family housing (hereinafter referred to as "management expenses, etc."), it shall comply with the following guidelines:

1. It shall select the business operator by electronic bidding: Provided, That where electronic bidding is not suitable to select the business operator, which is prescribed and publicly notified by the Minister of Land, Infrastructure and Transport, it may opt not to select the business operator by electronic bidding;
2. It shall follow methods prescribed by Presidential Decree, such as other bidding methods.

Article 26 (Audit)

(1) A management entity of multi-family housing with 300 or more households shall undergo an audit by an auditor (hereafter in this Article, referred to as "auditor") under Article 3 (1) of the Act on External Audit of Stock Companies at least once a year: Provided, That the foregoing shall not apply to the year in which the management entity obtains written consent from at least two-thirds of occupants, etc. of the relevant multi-family housing not to undergo the audit.

(2) In any of the following cases, the management entity of multi-family housing subject to compulsory management with less than 300 households shall undergo an audit by an auditor:

1. Where at least one-tenths of occupants, etc. requests an audit under the joint signature;
2. Where the council of occupants' representatives passes a resolution requesting an

audit.

(3) Where the management entity undergoes an audit pursuant to paragraph (1) or (2), it shall submit the results of the audit to the council of occupants' representatives within one month from the date it receives the results of the audit, such as an auditor's report, and disclose the results of the audit on the website of the relevant multi-family housing and the multi-family housing management information system.

(4) The council of occupants' representatives shall select an auditor to conducts an audit under paragraph (1) or (2). In such cases, the council of occupants' representatives may request the head of a Si/Gun/Gu or the Korean Institute of Certified Public Accountants under Article 41 of the Certified Public Accountant Act to recommend the auditor.

(5) No management entity which has undergone an audit pursuant to paragraph (1) or (2) shall engage in any of the following:

1. Refusing, interfering with or evading the auditor's request for perusal, reproduction or submission of data or his/her examination without just cause;
2. Interfering with the audit by unlawful means, such as submitting false data to the auditor.

(6) An auditor who conducts an audit under paragraph (1) or (2) shall submit the results of the audit to the head of a Si/Gun/Gu having jurisdiction over the relevant multi-family housing within one month from the date he/she completes the audit. *<Amended by Act No. 14709, Mar. 21, 2017>*

Article 27 (Preparation, Custody, Disclosure, etc. of Accounting Documents)

(1) The management entity of multi-family housing subject to compulsory management shall prepare books concerning all transactional activities, such as the collection, custody, deposit and disbursement of management expenses, on a monthly basis and keep such books along with evidential documents for five years from the end of the relevant fiscal year. In such cases, the management entity may prepare or keep books and evidential documents through the information processing system under subparagraph 2 of Article 2 of the Framework Act on Electronic Documents and Transactions.

(2) Where occupants, etc. request the perusal of books, evidential documents under paragraph (1) or other information prescribed by Presidential Decree, or the reproduction thereof at their own expenses, the management entity under paragraph (1) shall comply with such request, as prescribed by the management rules: Provided, That it shall comply with such request other than the following information:

1. Information likely to infringe on the privacy or rights of individuals, such as unique identifying information under Article 24 of the Personal Information Protection Act;
2. Information likely to cause substantial disruption to the fair performance of duties where such information, which is related to matters in the course of decision-making or internal review, is disclosed.

Article 28 (Disclosure of Written Contract)

Where the management entity of multi-family housing subject to compulsory management or the council of occupants' representatives enters into a contract with a housing management service provider selected pursuant to Article 7 (1) or a business operator who performs construction works, services etc. selected pursuant to Article 25, it shall disclose the written contract on the website of the relevant multi-family housing within one month from the date of conclusion of the contract. In such cases, it shall disclose the written contract other than information under Article 27 (2) 1.

Article 29 (Long-Term Repair Plan)

(1) A business entity who builds and supplies multi-family housing (including an owner of a building who builds facilities other than housing and housing in the same building after obtaining a building permit under Article 11 of the Building Act; hereafter in this Article, the same shall apply) falling under any of the following or a person who performs remodeling pursuant to Article 66 (1) and (2) of the Housing Act shall formulate a long-term repair plan for the common areas of such multi-family housing and submit such long-term repair plan to a person who has authority to

inspect the common areas for the use thereof when it requests such person to inspect the common areas for the use thereof (in case under subparagraph 4, referring to approval for use under Article 22 of the Building Act; hereafter in this Article, the same shall apply) under Article 49 of the Housing Act, and the person who has authority to inspect the common areas for the use thereof shall transfer the long-term repair plan to the management entity of the multi-family housing. In such cases, the person who has authority to inspect the common areas for the use thereof, may request the business entity or the person who performs remodeling to supplement the long-term repair plan: *<Amended by Act No. 13786, Jan. 19, 2016>*

1. Multi-family housing with 300 or more households;
2. Multi-family housing where elevators are installed;
3. Multi-family housing with the central heating system or the district heating system;
4. A building in which facilities other than housing and housing are built in the same building after obtaining a building permit under Article 11 of the Building Act.

(2) The council of occupants' representatives and the management entity shall examine a long-term repair plan every three years, and where necessary, adjust such long-term repair plan, as prescribed by Ordinance of the Ministry of Land, Infrastructure and Transport, and replace, maintain or repair important facilities in accordance with the long-term repair plan formulated or adjusted. In such cases, the council of occupants' representatives and the management entity shall record and keep matters examined concerning the long-term repair plan.

(3) Where the council of occupants' representatives and the management entity obtain written consent of a majority of all occupants because it is necessary in light of management conditions, such as the construction of important facilities, they may adjust a long-term repair plan before three years elapse.

(4) The management entity may require the head of the management office of the relevant multi-family housing to undergo education on the calculation of expenses in a long-term repair plan, methods of construction, etc. provided by the Mayor/Do Governor, as prescribed by Ordinance of the Ministry of Land, Infrastructure and Transport.

Article 30 (Accumulation of Reserves for Long - term Repairs)

(1) The management entity shall collect reserves for long-term repairs, necessary for the replacement, maintenance and repair of important facilities of multi-family housing and accumulate such reserves in accordance with a long-term repair plan.

(2) Reserves for long-term repairs shall be used in accordance with the relevant long-term repair plan: Provided, That where a majority of occupants of the relevant multi-family housing gives written consent, such reserves maty be used for the following purposes:

1. Expenses for mediation, etc. under Article 45;
2. Expenses incurred in inspecting and appraising defects under Article 48;
3. Expenses incurred in claiming expenses under subparagraph 1 or 2.

(3) Necessary matters concerning the scope of important facilities, timing, methods, etc. of the replacement, maintenance and repair thereof under paragraph (1) shall be prescribed by Ordinance of the Ministry of Land, Infrastructure and Transport.

(4) Necessary matters concerning the rate, methods of calculation, methods of accumulation, procedures for the use, post management, etc. of reserves for long-term repairs shall be prescribed by Presidential Decree.

Article 31 (Custody of Design Documents, etc.)

The management entity of multi-family housing subject to compulsory management shall have custody of design documents, etc. of multi-family housing, and record, keep and maintain the details of the replacement, maintenance, repair, etc. of facilities of multi-family housing for the systematic maintenance and management of multi-family housing, as prescribed by Presidential Decree.

Article 32 (Safety Management Plan, Education, etc.)

(1) The management entity of multi-family housing subject to compulsory management shall formulate a safety management plan and implement such safety management plan, designating a safety supervisor for each facility and a person responsible for

safety management in accordance with the safety management plan to prevent safety-related accidents occurring from facilities of the relevant multi-family housing, as prescribed by Presidential Decree.

(2) The following persons shall undergo crime prevention education and safety education provided by the head of a Si/Gun/Gu for the prevention of various safety-related accidents and crime prevention in multi-family housing, as prescribed by Ordinance of the Ministry of Land, Infrastructure and Transport:

1. Persons who engage in security guard service;
2. Persons selected as a safety supervisor of facilities and a person responsible for safety management in accordance with a safety management plan under paragraph (1).

(3) The head of a Si/Gun/Gu may provide crime prevention education and safety education by delegating or entrusting such education to an agency or corporation classified as follows, as prescribed by Ordinance of the Ministry of Land, Infrastructure and Transport:

1. Crime prevention education: The chief of the competent police station or a corporation recognized pursuant to Article 89 (2);
2. Safety education concerning firefighting: The chief of the competent fire station or a corporation recognized pursuant to Article 89 (2);
3. Safety education concerning facilities: A corporation recognized pursuant to Article 89 (2).

Article 33 (Safety Inspection)

(1) The management entity of multi-family housing subject to compulsory management shall conduct safety inspections of multi-family housing in accordance with methods, procedures, etc. for conducting safety inspections prescribed by guidelines under Article 13 (1) of the Special Act on the Safety Control of Establishments to protect occupants, etc. from accidents, disasters, etc. by maintaining functions and securing safety of such multi-family housing: Provided, That the management entity of multi-family housing subject to compulsory management shall require a person prescribed by Presidential Decree to conduct safety inspections of multi-family housing with 16 or more stories and multi-family housing with 15 or less stories prescribed by Presidential Decree in consideration of the number of years of use, the number of households, safety rating, the number of floors, etc. *<Amended by Act No. 13786, Jan. 19, 2016>*

(2) Where an accident or a disaster is likely to take place because the safety rating of the structure of buildings or facilities is very low as a result of safety inspections, the management entity under paragraph (1) shall immediately notify the council of occupants' representatives (in cases of rental housing, referring to a rental business operator; hereafter in this Article, the same shall apply) of the fact, report the fact to the head of a Si/Gun/Gu, as prescribed by Presidential Decree, and take necessary measures, such as restrictions on the use of the relevant building or the maintenance and repair thereof.

(3) The council of occupants' representatives and the management entity of multi-family housing subject to compulsory management shall secure a budget necessary for safety inspections of buildings and disaster prevention every year to secure the safety of the buildings and the public.

(4) Methods of safety inspections of multi-family housing, the timing of conducting safety inspections, equipment held for safety inspections and other matters necessary for safety inspections shall be prescribed by Presidential Decree.

Article 34 (Safety Management of Small-Scale Multi-Family Housing)

The head of a local government may conduct the following affairs for the management of multi-family housing which does not constitute multi-family housing subject to compulsory management and the prevention of safety-related accidents occurring from such multi-family housing:

1. Formulating and implementing a safety management plan for facilities under Article 32;
2. Safety inspections of multi-family housing under Article 33;

3. Other matters prescribed by Municipal Ordinance of a local government.

Article 35 (Criteria, etc. for Permission to Engage in Activities)

(1) Where an occupant, etc. or the management entity of multi-family housing (including welfare facilities sold to the general public; hereafter in this Article, the same shall apply) intends to engage in any activities falling under any of the following, he/she or it shall obtain permission from or make a report to the head of a Si/Gun/Gu in accordance with standards, procedures, etc. prescribed by Presidential Decree concerning the area, the number of households, the percentage of consent of occupants or occupants, etc. related to permission or a report:

1. Using multi-family housing other than for purposes under a project plan;
2. Extending, rebuilding or renovating multi-family housing (excluding remodeling under the housing Act);
3. Destroying or damaging multi-family housing or dismantling all or part of the relevant facilities (excluding insignificant activities prescribed by Ordinance of the Ministry of Land, Infrastructure and Transport);
4. Other activities prescribed by Presidential Decree, which interfere with the efficient management of multi-family housing.

(2) Article 19 of the Housing Act shall apply mutatis mutandis to matters under paragraph (1) permitted by or reported to the head of a Si/Gun/Gu concerning activities under paragraph (1) in consultation with the heads of related administrative agencies. *<Amended by Act No. 13786, Jan. 19, 2016>*

(3) Where an occupant, etc. or the management entity of multi-family housing intends to engage in any activities falling under any of the subparagraphs of paragraph (1) without permission or reporting, no person who performs construction works or consulting engineering services of multi-family housing shall perform construction works of or consulting engineering services for multi-family housing in cooperation with him/her or it in his/her or its activities. In such cases, a person who performs construction works of or consulting engineering services for multi-family housing shall pre-verify whether an occupant, etc. or the management entity has obtained permission or reported.

(4) Where the construction works is completed after an occupant, etc. or the management entity has obtained permission from or made a report to the head of a Si/Gun/Gu concerning activities under paragraph (1), he/she or it shall undergo an inspection for the use of multi-family housing, and Article 49 of the Housing Act shall apply mutatis mutandis to the inspection for the use thereof. *<Amended by Act No. 13786, Jan. 19, 2016>*

(5) Where a person who falls under paragraph (1) has obtained permission or made a report pursuant to paragraphs (1) and (2) by deception or other fraudulent means, the head of a Si/Gun/Gu may revoke his/her permission or acceptance of such report.

Article 36 (Warranty Liability for Defects)

(1) The following business entities (hereafter in this Chapter, referred to as "business entity") shall assume warranty liability (in case of a contractor under subparagraphs 3 and 4, referring to the contractor's warranty liability) for defects following the sale of multi-family housing. *<Amended by Act No. 14793, Apr. 18, 2017>*

1. Persons under the items of subparagraph 10 of Article 2 of the Housing Act;
2. An owner who has built multi-family housing for the purpose of sale after having obtained a building permit under Article 11 of the Building Act;
3. A contractor who has performed an act under Article 35 (1) 2;
4. A contractor who has performed remodelling under Article 66 of the Housing Act.

(2) Notwithstanding paragraph (1), a business entity under paragraph (1) 1, who supplies multi-family housing supplied for the purpose of conversion to the sale thereof after leasing multi-family housing (hereinafter referred to as "public rental housing") pursuant to subparagraph 1 (a) of Article 2 of the Special Act on Public Housing, shall assume warranty liability (excluding liability for damages under Article 37 (2)) for defects for lessees. *<Newly Inserted by Act No. 14793, Apr. 18, 2017>*

(3) The period for warranty liability (hereinafter referred to as "period for warranty

liability") under paragraphs (1) and (2) shall be prescribed by Presidential Decree within ten years for each load-bearing structure and each facility construction of multi-family housing in consideration of the importance of a defect, the durability period and possibility of replacement of facilities, etc. In such cases, the period for warranty liability shall be counted from the following dates: *<Amended by Act No. 13786, Jan. 19, 2016; Act No. 14793, Apr. 18, 2017>*

1. An area for exclusive use: Date on which possession is delivered to an occupant (in cases of warranty liability under paragraph (2), a lessee);
2. Common areas: Date of inspection for use under Article 49 of the Housing Act (where approval of the temporary use of the whole multi-family housing is obtained pursuant to the proviso to Article 49 (4) of the aforesaid Act, referring to the date of approval of the temporary use thereof, and where multi-family housing undergoes an inspection for the partial use thereof or inspection for the use of each building pursuant to the proviso to Article 49 (1) of the aforesaid Act, referring to the date of inspection for the partial use thereof or the date of inspection for the use of each building) or the date of approval to use of multi-family housing under Article 22 of the Building Act.

(4) Any defects under paragraph (1) (hereinafter referred to as "defects") means defects that may disrupt the safety, functions or light and outlook of buildings or structures because any crack, subsidence, damage, getting loose, leakage of water, etc. occurs due to construction defects, and the specific scope of defects shall be prescribed by Presidential Decree. *<Amended by Act No. 14793, Apr. 18, 2017>*

Article 37 (Repair of Defects, etc.)

(1) Where any defects are discovered during a period for warranty liability, the management entity (where a person who was awarded a lump sum contract for construction works by the management entity under Article 36 (1) and has performed construction works exists separately, who assumes warranty liability for defects pursuant to Article 28 of the Framework Act on the Construction Industry, referring to such person; hereafter in this Chapter, the same shall apply) shall repair such defects at the request of a person who falls under subparagraphs 1 through 4 of the relevant multi-family housing (hereafter in this Chapter, referred to as "council of occupants' representatives, etc.") or person who falls under subparagraph 5. In such cases, necessary matters concerning procedures for and completion of repairs of defects shall be prescribed by Presidential Decree: *<Amended by Act No. 14793, Apr. 18, 2017>*

1. Occupants;
2. The council of occupants' representatives;
3. The management entity (referring to the management entity that acts for occupants or the council of occupants' representatives concerning a request, etc. for repairing defects);
4. The management body under the Act on Ownership and Management of Condominium Buildings;
5. A lessee or the council of lessees' representatives (hereinafter referred to as "lessee, etc.") of public rental housing.

(2) Where any defect is discovered in multi-family housing during a period for warranty liability, a business entity shall be liable to compensate for damage caused by such defect. In such cases, Article 667 of the Civil Act shall apply mutatis mutandis to liability for damages. *<Amended by Act No. 14793, Apr. 18, 2017>*

(3) Where the head of a Si/Gun/Gu recognizes that important defects effect the safety of the structure of multi-family housing during a period for warranty liability, he/she may request a safety inspection agency to conduct safety inspections. In such cases, matters concerning structures subject to safety inspection, procedures for conducting safety inspections and the apportioning of expenses, and necessary matters concerning the range, etc. of safety inspection agencies shall be prescribed by Presidential Decree.

(4) Where a business entity fails to comply with a request for repair of defects made by the council of occupants' representatives, etc. and a lessee, etc. pursuant to

paragraph (1) without any justifiable reason, the head of a Si/Gun/Gu may order the business entity to take corrective action. *<Newly Inserted by Act No. 14793, Apr. 18, 2017>*

Article 38 (Putting up and Use of Security Deposit for Repairing Defects)

(1) The business entity shall put down a security deposit for repairing defects for the period for warranty liability (the warranty period shall be counted based on the common area) to guarantee the repair of defects, as prescribed by Presidential Decree: Provided, That the foregoing shall not apply to the State, local governments, the Korea Land and Housing Corporation and business entities which are local public corporations. *<Amended by Act No. 14793, Apr. 18, 2017>*

(2) The council of occupants' representatives, etc. shall use a security deposit for repairing defects under paragraph (1) only for purposes prescribed by Presidential Decree, such as expenses for repairing defects following a determination on defects by the Defect Examination and Dispute Mediation Committee under Article 39, and in cases of multi-family housing subject to compulsory management, the council of occupants' representatives, etc. shall report the details of the use of a security deposit for repairing defects to the head of a Si/Gun/Gu after using it, as prescribed by Ordinance of the Ministry of Land, Infrastructure and Transport.

(3) A person who receives a security deposit for repairing defects (hereinafter referred to as "institution that issues a letter of guarantee of a security deposit for repairing defects") under paragraph (1) shall notify the head of the relevant Si/Gun/Gu of the details of the payment of a security deposit for repairing defects within 30 days from the date he/she pays the security deposit for repairing defects to the council of occupants' representatives of multi-family housing subject to compulsory management, as prescribed by Ordinance of the Ministry of Land, Infrastructure and Transport. *<Newly Inserted by Act No. 14793, Apr. 18, 2017>*

(4) Necessary matters concerning the scope of placement and the custody of, demand for and payment of, the use and return of a security deposit for repairing defects under paragraph (1) shall be prescribed by Presidential Decree. *<Newly Inserted by Act No. 14793, Apr. 18, 2017>*

Article 39 (Establishment, etc. of Defect Examination and Dispute Mediation Committee)

(1) The Defect Examination and Dispute Mediation Committee (hereinafter referred to as the "Defect Dispute Mediation Committee") shall be established in the Ministry of Land, Infrastructure and Transport to examine, mediate and take charge of affairs under paragraph (2) related to warranty liability and repair of defects under Articles 36 through 38.

(2) Affairs of the Defect Dispute Mediation Committee shall be as follows: *<Amended by Act No. 14793, Apr. 18, 2017>*

1. Determining whether a defect exists;
2. Mediating disputes about warranty liability for defects, repair of defects, etc. among the business entity, an institution which has issued a letter of guarantee of a security deposit for repairing defects (hereinafter referred to as "business entity, etc.") and the council of occupants' representatives, etc., a lessee, etc.;
3. Mediating disputes about the scope, etc. of liability for defects among the business entity, etc., architects and consulting engineers;
4. Other matters prescribed by other statutes as affairs of the Defect Dispute Mediation Committee.

(3) A person who intends to file an application for examination of defects or mediation of a dispute (hereinafter referred to as "mediation, etc.") with the Defect Dispute Mediation Committee shall submit an application, as prescribed by Ordinance of the Ministry of Land, Infrastructure and Transport.

(4) Matters concerning methods of and standards for examination of defects necessary for mediation, etc. for which an application is filed pursuant to paragraph (3), methods of calculating expenses incurred in repairing defects, etc. shall be prescribed by Presidential Decree.

Article 40 (Composition, etc. of Defect Dispute Mediation Committee)

(1) The Defect Dispute Mediation Committee shall be comprised of not more than 50 members including one chairperson who is a regular full-time member. *<Amended by Act No. 14793, Apr. 18, 2017>*

(2) Subcommittees professionally dealing with determinations as to whether a defect exists or mediation of disputes shall be established in the Defect Dispute Mediation Committee, and each subcommittee shall be comprised of not less than 9 nor more than 15 members appointed by the Chairperson of the Defect Dispute Mediation Committee (hereinafter referred to as the "Chairperson").

(3) The Chairperson and chairpersons of subcommittees (hereinafter referred to as "chairperson of a subcommittee") shall be appointed by the Minister of Land, Infrastructure and Transport.

(4) The Chairperson may organize smaller committees, each of which is comprised of not less three nor more than five members, in consideration of specialized fields, etc. for examination, etc. of cases for each subcommittee. In such cases, the Chairperson shall appoint the chairpersons of smaller committees (hereinafter referred to as "chairperson of a smaller committee") from among members of the relevant subcommittee.

(5) Members of the Defect Dispute Mediation Committee shall be appointed or commissioned by the Minister of Land, Infrastructure and Transport from among those falling under any of the following, who have extensive knowledge and experience in defects of multi-family housing. In such cases, at least seven persons falling under subparagraph 3 shall be included in members of the Defect Dispute Mediation Committee: *<Amended by Act No. 14793, Apr. 18, 2017>*

1. Public officials equivalent to Class I through IV or public officials belonging to the Senior Executive Service or persons who hold the same position as the Senior Executive Service;
2. Persons who hold the office of at least associate professor, or a position equivalent thereto at a college or research institute officially recognized;
3. Persons who hold the office of judge, public prosecutor or attorney at law for at least six years;
4. Persons who have expert knowledge of construction works, electric works, telecommunications works, firefighting system installation, thorough safety inspection of structures or appraisal, and have engaged in such business for at least ten years;
5. Housing managers who have worked as the head of a management office of multi-family housing for at least ten years;
6. Certified architects who have reported pursuant to Article 23 (1) of the Certified Architects Act or professional engineers who registered pursuant to Article 6 (1) of the Professional Engineers Act, who have engaged in such business for at least ten years;
7. Deleted. *<by Act No. 14793, Apr. 18, 2017>*

(6) The term of office of the Chairperson and members who are not public officials shall be two years and they may serve a second consecutive term, and the term of office of a member who fills a vacancy shall be the remainder of the unexpired term of his/her predecessor.

(7) No member who is a not public official among members of the Defect Dispute Mediation Committee shall be dismissed against his/her will except in any of the following cases:

1. Where he/she is unable to perform his/her duties due to physical or mental disability;
2. Where he/she falls under any of the subparagraphs of Article 33 of the State Public Officials Act;
3. Where his/her behaviour constitutes grounds for dismissal prescribed by Presidential Decree, such as a violation of his/her duty.

(8) The Chairperson shall represent the Defect Dispute Mediation Committee and preside over its affairs: Provided, That where the Chairperson is unable to perform his/her

duties in extenuating circumstances, the chairpersons of subcommittees shall perform his/her duties in order of the Chairperson's appointment in advance.

Article 41 (Exclusion, etc. of Members)

(1) Where a member of the Defect Dispute Mediation Committee falls under any of the following, he/she shall be excluded from mediation, etc. of such case:

1. Where the member or his/her current or former spouse becomes the party to the relevant case or jointly holds the right or liability in the relevant case;
2. Where the member is or was a relative of the party to the relevant case;
3. Where the member testified in the relevant case, or has conducted an examination of defects or made an appraisal of defects under Article 48;
4. Where the member is or was involved in the relevant case as an agent of the party to the relevant case;
5. Where the member has been involved in measures or omission giving rise to the relevant case.

(2) Where the grounds for exclusion exists, the Defect Dispute Mediation Committee shall determine on exclusion on its own authority or at the request of the party.

(3) Where it is difficult for the parties to expect a member to perform a fair mediation, etc., he/she may file an application for challenge with the Defect Dispute Mediation Committee. Where the Defect Dispute Mediation Committee deems an application for challenge appropriate, it shall determine on challenge.

(4) Where a member's behaviour constitutes grounds under paragraph (1) or (3), he/she shall avoid mediation, etc. of such case of his/her own accord.

(5) The provisions of paragraphs (1) through (4) shall apply mutatis mutandis to employees of the organization for the operation of and conducting affairs of the Defect Dispute Mediation Committee under Article 49 (1) involved in procedures for mediation, etc.

Article 42 (Meetings, etc. of Defect Dispute Mediation Committee)

(1) The Chair person shall convene meetings of the committee of the whole, subcommittees and smaller committees, and the chairpersons of the relevant meetings shall be classified as follows:

1. The committee of the whole: The Chairperson;
2. Subcommittees: The chairperson of a subcommittee: Provided, That where the subcommittee considers matters prescribed by Presidential Decree, such as reconsideration under Article 43 (5), the Chairperson shall preside over meetings of the subcommittee;
3. Smaller committees: The chairperson of a smaller committee.

(2) The committee of the whole shall deliberate and determine on matters falling under the following. In such cases, the committee of the whole shall hold meetings when a majority of the incumbent members attends meetings, and pass resolutions with the consent of a majority of the members present:

1. Matters concerning the enactment, amendment and repeal of the rules concerning the proceedings of the Defect Dispute Mediation Committee;
2. Matters required by subcommittees to be deliberated and determined at meetings of the committee of the whole;
3. Other matters the Chairperson deems necessary.

(3) The subcommittees shall determine whether a defect exists or deliberate and determine on cases of the mediation of disputes, and hold meetings when a majority of its members attends meetings and pass resolutions with the consent of a majority of the members present. In such cases, matters determined by the subcommittee shall be deemed determined by the Defect Dispute Mediation Committee.

(4) The smaller committees shall deliberate and determine on matters falling under the following, conduct examinations, etc. of cases of the competent subcommittee, and hold a meeting when a majority of its members attend thereat and pass resolutions with the consent of all members present. In such cases, matters determined by the smaller committee shall be deemed determined by the Defect Dispute Mediation Committee:

1. Small claims cases;

2. Cases to be determined by the smaller committee determined by the subcommittee in consideration of specialized fields, etc.;
3. Rejection of an application for mediation, etc. under the latter part of Article 45 (2);
4. Cases on which both parties agree to accept a mediation plan of the smaller committee;
5. Other simple cases prescribed by Presidential Decree.

(5) Where the Defect Dispute Mediation Committee receives an application for mediation of a dispute, it may recommend the parties to reach agreement on the repair of defects, compensation for damage, etc. even while the mediation process is ongoing. In such cases, no recommendation shall have an influence on the ongoing mediation process.

(6) Necessary matters concerning the proceedings and operation, and rejection of mediation, etc. of the Defect Dispute Mediation Committee shall be prescribed by Presidential Decree. *<Amended by Act No. 14793, Apr. 18, 2017>*

Article 42-2 (Agents)

(1) A person who applies for mediation, etc. pursuant to Article 39 (3) and the other party thereto may appoint a person falling under any of the following as his/her agent:
1. An attorney-at-law;
2. The manager of the management body under Article 37 (1) 4;
3. The head of the management office under Article 64 (1);
4. A spouse of the relevant person or his/her relative within the fourth degree of consanguinity;
5. A user of a housing unit (limited to the exclusively possessed area);
6. Where the relevant person is the State or a local government, public officials belonging thereto;
7. Where the relevant person is a corporation, executive officers or employees of the corporation.

(2) An agent may act for the principal in the performance of the following acts only where the principal clearly expresses the fact that he/she specially authorize the agent to perform the following acts:
1. Withdrawal of an application;
2. Acceptance of a mediation agreement;
3. Appointment of a subagent.

(3) The authority of an agent shall be explained in writing.

[This Article Newly Inserted by Act No. 14793, Apr. 18, 2017]

Article 43 (Examination of Defects)

(1) The subcommittee that determines as to whether a defect exists pursuant to Article 42 (3) deems that it is appropriate to refer a case to the mediation of a dispute under Article 44 because expenses are excessively incurred in repairing the defect compared to the seriousness of the defect, it may send the case to the subcommittee that mediates a dispute and require the relevant subcommittee to mediate the relevant case after hearing the applicant's opinion, as prescribed by Presidential Decree. In such cases, no period required for examination of the defect shall be counted in the calculation of the period under Article 45 (1).

(2) Where the Defect Dispute Mediation Committee determines whether a defect exists, it shall mention matters prescribed by Presidential Decree in a written determination as to whether a defect exists and serve the original of such written determination as to whether a defect exists signed and sealed by the Chairperson on each person or his/her agent.

(3) Where the original of a written determination as to whether a defect exists is served on the business entity, etc. pursuant to paragraph (2), in which case it is determined that a defect exists (excluding where the result of a determination as to whether a defect exists has been altered pursuant to paragraph (7)), the business entity, etc. shall repair the defect, as prescribed by Presidential Decree.

(4) A person who has an objection to the result of a determination as to whether a defect exists under paragraph (2) may raise an objection accompanied by a written

opinion prepared by a specialized safety inspection agency under Article 48 (1) or a relevant expert prescribed by Presidential Decree within 30 days from the date a written determination as to whether a defect exists is served on him/her, as prescribed by Ordinance of the Ministry of Land, Infrastructure and Transport. *<Amended by Act No. 14793, Apr. 18, 2017>*

(5) Where an objection under paragraph (4) is raised, the Defect Dispute Mediation Committee shall require a subcommittee other than the subcommittee which has made a determination as to whether a defect exists under paragraph (2) to review the relevant case. In such cases, Article 45 (1) and (3) shall apply mutatis mutandis to the processing period.

(6) Where necessary to examine a case to which an objection is raised, the Defect Dispute Mediation Committee may request the parties and a safety inspection agency or a relevant expert that has prepared a written opinion under paragraph (4) to attend its meetings to make statements or to submit evidential material, etc. within a fixed period. In such cases, such safety inspection agency or relevant expert shall comply with such request.

(7) In order for the subcommittee that conducts reviews under paragraph (5) to alter the first determination as to whether a defect exists, it shall hold a meeting when a majority of its incumbent members attends the meeting and pass the resolution with the consent of at least two-thirds of the members present. In such cases, where at least two-thirds of the members present do not give consent, the first determination shall be deemed the final determination of the Defect Dispute Mediation Committee.

(8) Where the review is finalized pursuant to paragraph (7), the Defect Dispute Mediation Committee shall immediately serve the original of a written determination as to the review on each person or his/her agent.

Article 44 (Mediation of Disputes)

(1) Where the Defect Dispute Mediation Committee has completed procedures for mediation of a dispute under Article 39 (2) 2 and 3, it shall immediately determine a mediation plan stating matters prescribed by Presidential Decree, and present such mediation plan to each person or his/her agent.

(2) Each person to whom a mediation plan under paragraph (1) is presented shall notify the Defect Dispute Mediation Committee of his/her determination as to whether to accept such mediation plan within 30 days from the date the mediation plan is presented to him/her. In such cases, where he/she fails to make a reply to whether he/she accepts the mediation plan, he/she shall be deemed to have accepted the mediation plan.

(3) Where each person or his/her agent accepts a mediation plan (referring to where he/she accepts in writing or by electronic means, as prescribed by Presidential Decree) pursuant to paragraph (2) or fails to make a reply within the deadline, the Defect Dispute Mediation Committee shall immediately serve the original of a deed of mediation settlement signed and sealed by the Chairperson on each person or his/her agent.

(4) Content of a deed of mediation settlement under paragraph (3) has the same effect of a judicial conciliation: Provided, That the foregoing shall not apply to matters prescribed by Presidential Decree, which the relevant person cannot dispose of at his/her discretion.

Article 45 (Period, etc. for Handling of Disputes for Mediation, etc.)

(1) Upon receipt of an application for mediation, etc., the Defect Dispute Mediation Committee shall immediately begin procedures for mediation, etc. In such cases, it shall complete procedures for mediation within 60 days from the date it receives such application (in cases of a defect in the common areas, referring to 90 days, and the period for rectifying the defect under paragraph (2) and the period for assessing the defect under Article 48 shall not be included).

(2) Where a defect is discovered in the details of a case for which an application has been filed, the Defect Dispute Mediation Committee shall require an applicant to rectify such defect within a fixed period. In such cases, where the applicant fails to rectify the defect, it shall rule to reject the application for mediation, etc.

(3) Where the Defect Dispute Mediation Committee is unable to complete mediation, etc. within the period under paragraph (1), it may extend the period only once through a resolution of the subcommittee or the smaller committee in charge of the relevant case; such extension of period shall be up to 30 days. In such cases, it shall notify each person or his/her agent of the extension of the period in writing, specifying grounds therefor and the deadline.
(4) The Defect Dispute Mediation Committee may hear opinions of interested persons or a safety inspection agency, etc. that has examined defects pursuant to Article 48 (1) before it begins procedures for mediation, etc. under paragraph (1).
(5) Where additional expenses are incurred in conducting examinations, inspections, analysis of data, etc. in the process of mediation, etc., necessary matters concerning an entity who should subsidize expenses, methods of apportioning expenses, etc. shall be prescribed by Ordinance of the Ministry of Land, Infrastructure and Transport. *<Amended by Act No. 14793, Apr. 18, 2017>*
(6) A person who files an application for mediation, etc. with the Defect Dispute Mediation Committee shall pay a fee, as determined and publicly notified by the Minister of Land, Infrastructure and Transport. *<Amended by Act No. 14793, Apr. 18, 2017>*

Article 46 (Notification, etc. of Request for Mediation, etc.)
(1) Upon receipt of an application for mediation, etc. from one of the parties, the Defect Dispute Mediation Committee shall notify the other party of the details of such application.
(2) The other party who receives notification pursuant to paragraph (1) shall submit a written reply to the details of an application to the Defect Dispute Mediation Committee within ten days except in extenuating circumstances.
(3) The business entity, etc., architects, consulting engineers, the council of occupants' representatives, etc., and lessees, etc. that have received notification concerning an application for mediation, etc. from the Defect Dispute Mediation Committee shall respond to mediation of a dispute: Provided, That where occupants (in cases of public rental housing, referring to lessees) who have received notification concerning an application for mediation, etc. fail to attend mediation on the date set therefor, the Defect Dispute Mediation Committee may determine a mediation plan by inherent authority pursuant to Article 44 (1), and present such mediation plan to each person or his/her agent. *<Amended by Act No. 13676, Dec. 29, 2015; Act No. 14793, Apr. 18, 2017>*
(4) Necessary matters concerning notification of the date of mediation and the date of examination of the Defect Dispute Mediation Committee, attendance of relevant persons and interested persons, the representatives selected, registration of the results of the implementation of mediation, etc. shall be prescribed by Presidential Decree. *<Newly Inserted by Act No. 14793, Apr. 18, 2017>*

Article 47 (Application Mutatis Mutandis of Judicial Conciliation of Civil Disputes Act, etc.)
(1) The Defect Dispute Mediation Committee shall apply the Judicial Conciliation of Civil Disputes Act mutatis mutandis to matters not otherwise expressly prescribed by this Act concerning procedures for mediation, etc. of disputes and the suspension of extinctive prescription.
(2) The provisions of Articles 174 through 197 of the Civil Procedure Act shall apply mutatis mutandis to service of documents following mediation, etc.

Article 48 (Examinations and Assessments of Defects)
(1) Where the business entity, etc. has an objection to a request for repairing defects made by the council of occupants' representatives, etc. or a lessee, etc. under Article 37 (1), it may entrust an examination of defects, such as whether any defects fall within the scope of defects which it is responsible for repairing, to a safety inspection agency prescribed by Presidential Decree in consultation with the council of occupants' representatives, etc. or a lessee, etc. In such cases, the safety inspection agency entrusted with the examination of defects shall immediately examine defects and notify the business entity, etc. and the council of occupants'

representatives, etc. or a lessee, etc. of the result of the examination thereof. *<Amended by Act No. 14793, Apr. 18, 2017>*

(2) In any of the following cases, the Defect Dispute Mediation Committee may request a safety inspection agency prescribed by Presidential Decree to conduct assessments of the cases:

1. Cases on which the parties dispute about the result of the examination of defects under paragraph (1);
2. Cases on which both parties or one party request(s) the assessment of defects;
3. Cases on which the cause of a defect is unclear;
4. Other cases on which the Defect Dispute Mediation Committee determines that assessment of defects are necessary.

(3) Expenses incurred in examining defects under paragraph (1) and expenses incurred in conducting assessments under paragraph (2) shall be borne by the parties, as prescribed by Ordinance of the Ministry of Land, Infrastructure and Transport.

Article 49 (Entrustment of Operation of and Management of Affairs of Defect Dispute Mediation Committee)

(1) The Minister of Land, Infrastructure and Transport may entrust the operation of and management of affairs of the Defect Dispute Mediation Committee to Korea Infrastructure Safety and Technology Corporation (hereafter in this Article, referred to as "Korea Infrastructure Safety and Technology Corporation") under Article 25 of the Special Act on the Safety Control of Establishments. In such cases, necessary matters concerning the organization (hereinafter referred to as the "Secretariat of the Defect Dispute Mediation Committee"), human resources, etc. for the operation of and management of affairs of the Defect Dispute Mediation Committee shall be prescribed by Presidential Decree.

(2) The Minister of Land, Infrastructure and Transport may fund or subsidize expenses for the operation of and management of affairs of the Defect Dispute Mediation Committee to Korea Infrastructure Safety and Technology Corporation within the budget.

Article 50 (Non-Disclosure, etc. of Procedures)

(1) Procedures for mediation, etc. and decision-making process which the Defect Dispute Mediation Committee performs shall not be disclosed: Provided, That the foregoing shall not apply where the subcommittee and the smaller committee determines to make disclosure.

(2) No member of the Defect Dispute Mediation Committee and no person who performs or performed affairs of the Secretariat of the Defect Dispute Mediation Committee as its employee shall divulge confidential information they became aware of in the course of performing mediation, etc.

Article 51 (Examination, Inspection, etc. of Facts)

(1) Upon receipt of an application for mediation, etc., the Chairperson of the Defect Dispute Mediation Committee may require employees of the Secretariat of the Defect Dispute Mediation Committee to examine or inspect and peruse matters subject to examination or mediation and relevant data, or to hear statements of unsworn witnesses. In such cases, the business entity, etc., the council of occupants' representatives, etc. and a lessee, etc. shall provide cooperation in the aforesaid activities. *<Amended by Act No. 14793, Apr. 18, 2017>*

(2) A person who conducts examinations, inspections, etc. pursuant to paragraph (1) shall carry a certificate of identification indicating his/her authority and produce such certificate to the relevant persons.

Article 52 (Registration of Housing Management Services)

(1) A person who intends to provide housing management services shall register housing management services with the head of a Si/Gun/Gu, as prescribed by Presidential Decree, and where any registered matters are altered, he/she shall report alterations, as prescribed by Ordinance of the Ministry of Land, Infrastructure and Transport.

(2) No housing management service provider who registered pursuant to paragraph (1) shall be registered within two years after his/her registration is cancelled pursuant to Article 53.

(3) A housing manager (including a corporation at least one-thirds of the executives or employees of which are housing managers) may apply for registration under paragraph (1). In such cases, a person who intends to register housing management services shall meet the following requirements:
1. Capital (where the person is not a corporation, referring to the appraised value of assets) shall be more than the amount prescribed by Presidential Decree, which shall be at least 200 million won;
2. The person shall have human resources, facilities and equipment prescribed by Presidential Decree.

(4) Other necessary matters, such as procedures for registering a housing management service provider, types of business, methods of the management of multi-family housing, and the details of its affairs, shall be prescribed by Presidential Decree.

(5) No person other than a housing management service provider shall use "housing management services" or similar in a business name.

(6) Except as otherwise expressly provided for in this Act, the provisions concerning delegation of the Civil Act shall apply mutatis mutandis to the status of a housing management services provider.

Article 53 (Cancellation, etc. of Registration of Housing Management Services)

(1) Where a housing management service provider falls under any of the following, the head of a Si/Gun/Gu shall cancel his/her registration or order him/her to suspend all or some of his/her services for a fixed period of up to one year: Provided, That where he/she falls under subparagraph 1, 2 or 9, the head of a Si/Gun/Gu shall cancel his/her registration, and where he/she falls under subparagraph 7 or 8, the head of a Si/Gun/Gu shall order him/her to suspend all or some of his/her services for a fixed period up to one year:
1. Where he/she has registered by fraud or other improper means;
2. Where he/she provides housing management services during a period for suspension of business or he/she has been subjected to the suspension of business at least two times for the last three years and the total period for suspension of business exceeds 12 months;
3. Where he/she has caused property damage to owners and/or users because he/she has mismanaged multi-family housing by intention or gross negligence;
4. Where the results of the management of multi-family housing do not meet criteria prescribed by Presidential Decree;
5. Where he/she fails to meet any requirements for registration under Article 52 (3);
6. Where he/she manages multi-family housing, in violation of methods of management, the details of affairs, etc. under Article 52 (4);
7. Where he/she unlawfully acquires or provides a fortune or profit from property, in violation of Article 90 (2);
8. Where he/she uses management expenses, user fees and reserves for long-term repairs other than purposes under this Act, in violation of Article 90 (3);
9. Where he/she permits another person to provide service or conduct affairs prescribed by this Act using his/her name or trade name, or lends his/her registration certificate, in violation of Article 90 (4);
10. Where he/she refuses, interferes with or evades a report, submission of data, examination or inspection under Article 93 (1), or makes a false report;
11. Where he/she refuses, interferes with or evades an audit under Article 93 (3) and (4).

(2) Where a housing management service provider falls under any of paragraph (1) 3 through 6, 10 and 11, the head of a Si/Gun/Gu may impose an administrative fine of not more than ten million won in lieu of the suspension of business, as prescribed by Presidential Decree.

(3) Where a housing management service provider fails to pay an administrative fine by the deadline under paragraph (2), the head of a Si/Gun/Gu shall collect the administrative fine pursuant to the Act on the Collection, etc. of Local Non-Tax Revenue.

(4) Necessary matters concerning guidelines for the cancellation of registration and the

suspension of business under paragraph (1) and the amounts, etc. of administrative fines based on types of violations on which administrative fines under paragraph (2) are imposed and the level of violation shall be prescribed by Presidential Decree.

Article 63 (Duties, etc. of Management Entity)

(1) The management entity shall perform the following duties. In such cases, the management entity may use the common areas of multi-family housing to the necessary extent:

1. Maintenance, repair and safety management of the common areas of multi-family housing;
2. Security guard service, cleaning, disinfection and garbage collection within a multi-family housing complex;
3. Collection of management expenses and user fees and payment of public utility charges, etc. on behalf of occupants, etc.;
4. Collection, accumulation and management of reserves for long-term repairs;
5. Conducting matters prescribed by the management rules;
6. Conducting matters determined by the council of occupants' representatives;
7. Other matters prescribed by Ordinance of the Minister of Land, Infrastructure and Transport.

(2) The management entity shall manage multi-family housing pursuant to this Act or an order under this Act.

Article 64 (Duties, etc. of Head of Management Office)

(1) A person who manages multi-family housing subject to compulsory management, who falls under any of the following, shall assign a housing manager to the head of the management office of the relevant multi-family housing (hereinafter referred to as "head of the management office"): Provided, That in cases of multi-family housing with the number of households less than that prescribed by Presidential Decree, the person may assign a probationary housing manager as the head of the management office of the relevant multi-family housing, in lieu of a housing manager:

1. Council of occupants' representatives (limited to cases of autonomous management);
2. The business entity before it transfers its management duties pursuant to Article 13 (1);
3. The housing management service provider;
4. The rental business operator.

(2) The head of the management office shall perform the following duties to protect the rights and interests of occupants, etc. of multi-family housing through the safe and efficient management of multi-family housing:

1. The following duties determined by the council of occupants' representatives:
   (a) Operation, management, maintenance, repair, replacement and improvement of multi-family housing;
   (b) Duties to charge, receive and disburse management expenses, reserves for long-term repairs or other expenses, and manage the source of such funds to conduct duties under subparagraph 1.
2. Duties concerning the discovery of defects, requests for repairing defects, adjustment of a long-term repair plan, the formulation of a facility safety management plan and safety inspection of buildings: Provided, That matters accompanied by the disbursement of expenses shall be subject to determination by the council of occupants' representatives;
3. Superintendence and comprehensive management of duties of the management office;
4. Other duties prescribed by Ordinance of the Ministry of Land, Infrastructure and Transport concerning the management of multi-family housing.

(3) The head of the management office may perform judicial or extrajudicial actions on behalf of the council of occupants' representatives in relation to paragraph (2) 1 (a) and (b).

(4) The head of the management office shall perform his/her duties by paying attention of his/her fiduciary duty.

(5) The head of the management office shall report his/her assignment and an official

seal to be used in the performance of his/her duties to the head of a Si/Gun/Gu, as prescribed by Ordinance of the Ministry of Land, Infrastructure and Transport. The foregoing shall also apply where any alterations are made to his/her assignment and the official seal reported.

Article 65 (Preclusion, etc. of Unreasonable Intereference in Duties of Head of Management Office)

(1) No council of occupants' representatives (including its members; hereinafter the same shall apply) shall unreasonably interfere with the head of the management office performing duties under Article 64 (2).

(2) Where the council of occupants' representatives causes or is likely to cause losses to occupants, etc. through its unreasonable interference in the head of the management office performing duties, the head of the management office may report the fact to the head of a Si/Gun/Gu and request him/her to make an examination of the fact.

(3) Where the head of a Si/Gun/Gu is requested to make an examination of the fact pursuant to paragraph (2), he/she shall immediately make the examination thereof, and where he/she deems the council of occupants' representatives has unreasonably interfered in the head of the management office performing duties, he/she shall take measures, such as the issuance of a necessary order to the council of occupants' representatives, pursuant to Article 93.

(4) The head of a Si/Gun/Gu shall notify the head of the management office of the result of the examination of the fact or the result of taking measures, such as an order to make corrections.

(5) No council of occupants' representatives shall dismiss the head of the management office or request a housing management service provider to dismiss him/her on the pretext of a report or a request for examining the fact under paragraph (2) or an order, etc. under paragraph (3).

(6) Occupants, etc., the council of occupants' representatives, the management entity, etc. shall endeavor to pay an adequate salary to workers, such as security guards, and improve the treatment of workers and respect their human rights, and shall not give inappropriate instructions or orders to workers other than their duties. *<Amended by Act No. 14709, Mar. 21, 2017>*

(7) Workers, such as security guards, shall provide labor services of a high standards to occupants, etc.

Article 66 (Liability to Pay Compensation for Damage by Head of Management Office)

(1) Where a housing manager, etc. causes property damage to occupants, etc. intentionally or by negligence while performing the duties of the head of the management office, he/she shall be liable to compensate for such damage.

(2) In order to indemnify the liability to pay compensation for damage under paragraph (1), a housing manager, etc. shall take out guarantee insurance, join a mutual aid program or make a deposit under Article 82, as prescribed by Presidential Decree.

(3) After a housing manager, etc. has taken out guarantee insurance, joined a mutual aid program or made a deposit to indemnify the liability to pay compensation for damage under paragraph (2), he/she shall submit a document proving that he/she has taken out guarantee insurance, etc. to a person falling under any of the following on the date he/she is assigned to the head of the management office of the relevant multi-family housing:

1. Chairperson of the council of occupants' representatives;
2. In cases of rental housing, a rental business operator;
3. Where no council of occupants' representatives exists, the head of a Si/Gun/Gu.

(4) No money deposited pursuant to paragraph (2) shall be withdrawn within three years from the date a housing manager, etc. resigns from office as the head of the management office of the relevant multi-family housing, is dismissed from the office or dies.

Article 67 (Qualification of Housing Managers)

(1) A person who intends to become a probationary housing manager shall be issued a certificate upon passing a qualifying examination from the Mayor/Do Governor *[in cases of a large city with a population of at least 500,000 (hereinafter referred to as*

"large city") excluding the Seoul Metropolitan City, Metropolitan Cities and Special Self-Governing Cities under Article 175 of the Local Autonomy Act, referring to its Mayor; hereinafter the same shall apply through Article 70] after he/she passes the qualifying examination conducted by the Minister of Land, Infrastructure and Transport.

(2) A housing manager shall be a person who meets the following requirements and has been issued a qualification certificate of housing manager from the Mayor/Do Governor:

1. He/she shall hold a certificate upon passing the qualifying examination for probationary housing managers pursuant to paragraph (1);
2. He/she shall have work experience related to housing prescribed by Presidential Decree.

(3) Necessary matters concerning procedures for the issuance of a qualification certificate of housing manager under paragraph (2) shall be prescribed by Presidential Decree.

(4) No person who falls under any of the following shall become a housing manager, etc. and he/she shall become disqualified accordingly:

1. A person under adult guardianship or a person under limited guardianship;
2. A person declared bankrupt who is yet unreinstated;
3. A person in whose case two years have not passed since his/her imprisonment without labor or heavier punishment was completely executed (including where the execution thereof is deemed completed) or exempted as declared by a court;
4. A person who is subject to a suspended sentence of the imprisonment without labor or heavier punishment as declared by a court;
5. A person in whose case three years have not passed since his/her qualification as a housing manager, etc. was revoked (excluding where his/her qualification as a housing manager, etc. was revoked because he/she fell under subparagraphs 1 and 2).

(5) The Minister of Land, Infrastructure and Transport shall determine the number of persons to be selected through a qualifying examination for probationary housing managers of the relevant year in consideration of the number of multi-family housing complexes regarding approval of a project plan was granted for the immediately preceding three years, the number of persons who applied for qualifying examinations for probationary housing managers for the immediately preceding three years, the current status of employment of housing managers, etc., opinion of the committee on examinations for probationary housing managers on its deliberation under Article 68, etc. In such cases, the Minister of Land, Infrastructure and Transport shall determine persons who have passed the qualifying examination for probationary housing manager in order of top scorers in total marks of all subjects, who have earned marks higher than passing marks prescribed by Presidential Decree within the number of persons to be selected. *<Newly Inserted by Act No. 14093, Mar. 22, 2016>*

(6) Qualification to apply for qualifying examinations for probationary housing managers under paragraph (1), examination subjects, partial exemption from examination, an examination fee, and other matters necessary for examination shall be prescribed by Presidential Decree. *<Amended by Act No. 14093, Mar. 22, 2016>*

Article 68 (Committee on Examinations for Probationary Housing Managers)

(1) The committee on examinations for probationary housing managers may be established in the Ministry of Land, Infrastructure and Transport to deliberate on the following related to qualifying examinations for probationary housing managers under Article 67 (1):

1. Matters concerning examinations, such as the adjustment of subjects for qualifying examinations for probationary housing managers;
2. Matters concerning the number of persons to be selected at examinations and determination of standards for passing qualifying examinations;
3. Other important matters related to qualifying examinations for probationary housing managers.

(2) Necessary matters concerning composing, operating, etc. the committee on

examinations for probationary housing managers shall be prescribed by Presidential Decree.

Article 69 (Revocation, etc. of Qualification of Housing Managers, etc.)

(1) Where a housing manager, etc. falls under any of the following, the Mayor/Do Governor may revoke his/her qualification or suspend his/her qualification for a fixed period not exceeding one year: Provided, That where he/she falls under any of subparagraphs 1 through 4 and 7, the Mayor/Do Governor shall revoke his/her qualification: *<Amended by Act No. 13786, Jan. 19, 2016>*

1. Where he/she obtains a qualification by fraud or other improper means;
2. Where he/she has been sentenced to imprisonment without labor or heavier punishment in relation to managerial affairs of multi-family housing;
3. Where a housing manager, etc. who was employed for multi-family housing subject to compulsory management is employed for other multi-family housing, and facilities other than housing, such as a shopping mall or an officetel;
4. Where a housing manager, etc. conducts managerial affairs of multi-family housing during a period for suspension of qualification;
5. Where a housing manager, etc. causes property damage to owners and users by mismanaging multi-family housing intentionally or by gross negligence;
6. Where a housing manager, etc. obtains unjust enrichment, such as bribery, in relation to his/her duties;
7. Where a housing manager, etc. requires another person to perform duties prescribed by this Act using his/her name or lends his/her qualification certificate in violation of Article 90 (4);
8. Where a housing manager, etc. refuses, interferes with or evades a report, submission of data, an examination or inspection under Article 93 (1), or makes a false report;
9. Where a housing manager, etc. refuses, interferes with or avades an audit under Article 93 (3) and (4).

(2) Criteria for the revocation and suspension of qualification under paragraph (1) shall be prescribed by Presidential Decree.

Article 70 (Education of Housing Management Service Providers, etc.)

(1) A housing management service provider (in cases of a corporation, referring to the representative thereof) and a housing manager, etc. assigned to the head of the management office shall undergo education concerning the management of multi-family housing and ethics education from the Mayor/Do Governor. In such cases, a housing manager, etc. who intends to be assigned to the head of the management office may undergo education concerning the management of multi-family housing and ethics education, as prescribed by Ordinance of the Ministry of Land, Infrastructure and Transport, and where he/she has received such education, he/she shall be deemed to have performed his/her obligation to undergo education as the head of the management office.

(2) Where a housing manager, etc. who intends to be assigned to the head of the management office has no career experience as a head of the management office, an employee of a management body of multi-family housing or an executive officer or employee of a housing management service provider within the immediately preceding five years from the scheduled date of assignment, he/she may be assigned to the head of the management office after he/she completes education concerning the management of multi-family housing and ethics education conducted by the Mayor/Do Governor, as prescribed by Ordinance of the Ministry of Land, Infrastructure and Transport. In such cases, the housing manager, etc. who is assigned to the head of the management office after he/she completes education concerning the management of multi-family housing and ethics education shall be deemed to have performed obligation to undergo education as the head of the management office.

(3) A housing manager, etc. who is working as the head of the management office of multi-family housing after assigned to the office shall undergo education concerning the management of multi-family housing and ethics education every three years after

he/she receives education under paragraph (1) or (2), as prescribed by Ordinance of the Ministry of Land, Infrastructure and Transport.

(4) The Minister of Land, Infrastructure and Transport may prepare and implement guidelines necessary for education standards, methods of education, etc. to maintain the nationwide balance of education conducted by Mayors/Do Governors pursuant to paragraphs (1) through (3).

Article 71 (Establishment of Multi-Family Housing Management Dispute Mediation Committee)

(1) The Central Multi-Family Housing Management Dispute Mediation Committee (hereinafter referred to as the "Central Dispute Mediation Committee") shall be established within the Ministry of Land, Infrastructure and Transport to mediate disputes about the management of multi-family housing (excluding disputes related to warranty liability for repairs, repairs of defects, etc. of multi-family housing under Articles 36 and 37; hereafter in this Chapter, the same shall apply), and a regional multi-family housing management dispute meditation committee (hereinafter referred to as "regional multi-family housing management dispute meditation committee") shall be established within each Si/Gun/Gu (referring to an autonomous Gu; hereinafter the same shall apply): Provided, That in cases of a Si/Gun/Gu recognized by the Minister of Land, Infrastructure and Transport, with a low percentage of multi-family housing, a regional multi-family housing management dispute meditation committee may not be established within such Si/Gun/Gu.

(2) A multi-family housing management dispute meditation committee shall deliberate on and mediate the following:

1. Matters concerning composing and operating the council of occupants' representatives, and qualification, appointment, dismissal, and the term of office of representatives of each building;
2. Matters concerning composing and operating a management body of multi-family housing;
3. Matters concerning collecting, using, etc. management expenses, user fees and reserves for long-term repairs;
4. Matters concerning maintaining, repairing, improving, etc. multi-family housing (applicable only to the common areas);
5. Matters concerning remodeling multi-family housing;
6. Matters concerning noise from human activities in upper living spaces of multi-family housing;
7. Matters concerning disputes in a mixed housing complex;
8. Matters prescribed by other statutes about which the multi-family housing management dispute meditation committee may deliberate on and mediate disputes;
9. Other matters prescribed by Presidential Decree or Ordinance of a Si/Gun/Gu (limited to a regional dispute mediation committee) about which deliberation or mediation of disputes is necessary in relation to the management of multi-family housing.

Article 72 (Jurisdiction over Affairs of Central Dispute Mediation Committee and Regional Dispute Mediation Committees)

(1) The Central Dispute Mediation Committee shall deliberate on and mediate the following among matters under the subparagraphs of Article 71 (2):

1. Disputes spread over areas under the jurisdiction of at least two Sis/Guns/Gus;
2. Where no regional dispute mediation committee is established within a Si/Gun/Gu, disputes under the jurisdiction of the relevant Si/Gun/Gu;
3. Disputes for the mediation of which the parties to a dispute file an application with the Central Dispute Mediation Committee under the mutual agreement;
4. Other disputes prescribed by Presidential Decree over which it is necessary for the Central Dispute Mediation Committee to exercise jurisdiction.

(2) A regional dispute mediation committee shall deliberate on and mediate disputes other than disputes subject to deliberation and mediation by the Central Dispute Mediation Committee under paragraph (1), among disputes which have arisen within

the jurisdiction of the relevant Si/Gun/Gu.

Article 73 (Composition etc. of Central Dispute Mediation Committee)

(1) The Central Dispute Mediation Committee shall be comprised of not more than 15 members including one Chairperson.

(2) The Minister of Land, Infrastructure and Transport shall appoint or commission members of the Central Dispute Mediation Committee from among those who fall under any of the following, who have extensive knowledge and experience in the management of multi-family housing. In such cases, at least three persons falling under subparagraph 3 shall be included in the members thereof:

1. Public officials whose positions are equivalent to Grade I through IV or public officials belonging to the Senior Executive Service;
2. Persons who hold the office of associate professor or higher office at a officially recognized college or hold office equivalent thereto at a research institute;
3. Persons who have held the office of judge, public prosecutor or attorney-at-law for at least six years;
4. Persons who are qualified as certified public accountants, certified tax accountants, certified architects, certified public appraisers or certified public labor attorneys, who have worked in the relevant jobs for at least ten years;
5. Persons who are housing managers, who have worked as the head of the management office of multi-family housing for at least ten years;
6. Other persons prescribed by Presidential Decree, who have expert knowledge in the management of multi-family housing.

(3) Article 40 (3), (6) and (7) shall apply mutatis mutandis to the appointment of the Chairperson of the Central Dispute Mediation Committee, matters concerning the term of office and consecutive service of members who are not public officials, the term of office of members who have filled vacancies, the right of members who are not public officials not to be subject to dismissal against their will, respectively.

(4) Article 40 (8) shall apply mutatis mutandis to duties of the Chairperson of the Central Dispute Mediation Committee or the performance of his/her duties on his/her behalf where he/she is unable to perform his/her duties in extenuating circumstances. In such cases, the "chairperson of the subcommittee" in Article 40 (8) shall be construed as a "member".

(5) Article 41 shall apply mutatis mutandis to exclusion, challenge or voluntary refrainment of a member of the Central Dispute Mediation Committee.

(6) The Central Dispute Mediation Committee shall hold meetings when a majority of the incumbent members attends meetings, and pass resolutions with the consent of a majority of the members present.

(7) The Central Dispute Mediation Committee may prescribe procedures for handling affairs under its jurisdiction, and rules concerning the operation thereof.

(8) Necessary matters concerning composing, operating etc. the Central Dispute Mediation Committee shall be prescribed by Presidential Decree.

Article 74 (Request for Mediation of Disputes, Mediation, etc.)

(1) Where a dispute about matters under the subparagraphs of Article 71 (2) arises, an application for mediation may be filed with the Central Dispute Mediation Committee.

(2) Upon receipt of an application for mediation pursuant to paragraph (1), the Central Dispute Mediation Committee shall begin procedures for mediation immediately. In such cases, where the Central Dispute Mediation Committee deems it necessary, it may require the parties or interested persons to attend its meetings to hear their opinions.

(3) The Central Dispute Mediation Committee shall prepare a mediation plan and present it to each party immediately after it completes procedures for mediation under paragraph (2) within 30 days from the date it begins such procedures: Provided, That where it is unable to complete procedures for mediation within 30 days in extenuating circumstances, it may extend such period. In such cases, it shall notify the parties of the extension of the period in writing, specifying the reason therefor and the extended period.

(4) The the parties who receive a mediation plan shall notify the Central Dispute Mediation Committee as to whether they accept such mediation plan in writing within 30 days from the date they receive the mediation plan. In such cases, where they fail to express their intention within 30 days, they shall be deemed to have accepted the mediation plan.

(5) Where the parties accept or are deemed to have accepted a mediation plan, the Central Dispute Mediation Committee shall prepare a deed of mediation settlement and immediately serve the original of the deed of mediation settlement on each party or his/her agent after the Chairperson and each party sign and seal the deed of mediation settlement: Provided, That where the parties are deemed to have accepted the deed of mediation settlement, the signature and seal of each party may be omitted.

(6) Where the parties accept or are deemed to have accepted a mediation plan pursuant to paragraph (5), the content of such deed of mediation settlement shall have the same effect as a judicial conciliation: Provided, That the foregoing shall not apply to matters for which the parties are unable to take measures at their discretion.

(7) Necessary matters concerning procedures and methods for applying for mediation, the apportioning of expenses, etc. shall be prescribed by Ordinance of the Ministry of Land, Infrastructure and Transport.

Article 75 (Notification, etc. of Request for Mediation of Disputes)

(1) Article 46 (1) and (2) shall apply mutatis mutandis to the duty of the Central Dispute Mediation Committee to notify the other party of an application for mediation of a dispute, and the duty of the other party that receives notification of such application to submit a written reply, respectively.

(2) The council of occupants' representatives (including its members) and the management entity that receive notification of an application for mediation of a dispute from the Central Dispute Mediation Committee shall participate in mediation of the dispute.

Article 76 (Fact - Finding Examination, Inspection, etc.)

(1) The Central Dispute Mediation Committee may require its members or employees of an organization for the operation of and conducting affairs of the Central Dispute Mediation Committee (hereinafter referred to as the "Secretariat of the Central Dispute Mediation Committee") under Article 79 (2) to have access to the relevant multi-family housing, etc., to conduct examinations, inspections and have perusal, or to hear statements of unsworn witnesses. In such cases, the parties and interested persons shall provide cooperation in their activities.

(2) A person who conducts examinations, inspections, etc. pursuant to paragraph (1) shall carry a certificate of identification indicating his/her authority and produce it to the relevant persons.

Article 77 (Refusal and Suspension of Mediation)

(1) Where the Central Dispute Mediation Committee deems that it is inappropriate for the Central Dispute Mediation Committee to mediate a dispute in light of the nature of such dispute or deems that an application for mediation has been filed for vexatious purposes, it may refuse to mediate the same. In such cases, it shall notify an applicant of the reason for refusal of mediation.

(2) Where one party files a lawsuit while procedures for handling a case of which an application for mediation has been filed are being followed, the Central Dispute Mediation Committee shall suspend the process of mediation and notify the parties of the suspension thereof.

(3) Article 42 (5) shall apply mutatis mutandis to recommendations made by the Central Dispute Mediation Committee to reach an agreement during procedures for its mediation for the parties of a dispute.

Article 78 (Application Mutatis Mutandis, etc. of Judicial Conciliation of Civil Disputes Act, etc.)

@Articles 47 and 50 shall apply mutatis mutandis to the application of the Judicial Conciliation of Civil Dispute Act mutatis mutandis to the suspension of extinctive pre-scription of the Central Dispute Mediation Committee, service of documents, procedures, non-disclosure of decision-making process and the prohibition of divulgence of con-fidential information it has obtained officially.

Article 79 (Operation of Central Dispute Mediation Committee and Entrustment of Conducting Affairs)

(1) The Minister of Land, Infrastructure and Transport may entrust the operation of and the conducting of affairs of the Central Dispute Mediation Committee to an institution or organization designated through an announcement.

(2) Necessary matters concerning the organization, human resources, etc. for operation of and conducting of affairs of the Central Dispute Mediation Committee under paragraph (1) shall be prescribed by Presidential Decree.

(3) The Minister of Land, Infrastructure and Transport may fund or subsidize expenses incurred in operating the Central Dispute Mediation Committee and conducting its affairs to an entrusted institution or organization under paragraph (1) within the budget.

Article 80 (Regional Dispute Mediation Committees)

(1) The provisions concerning the Central Dispute Mediation Committee shall apply mutatis mutandis to the right of members who are not public officials, the members of a regional dispute mediation committee not to be subject to dismissal against their will, and the details concerning exclusion, challenge and voluntary refrainment of members.

(2) Where the parties to a dispute accept the result of mediation of a regional dispute mediation committee, an agreement of the same content as the protocol of mediation between the parties shall be deemed reached.

(3) Necessary matters concerning composing a regional dispute mediation committee shall be prescribed by Presidential Decree, and necessary matters concerning meetings, the operation, etc. of a regional dispute mediation committee shall be prescribed by Ordinance of the relevant Si/Gun/Gu.

Article 81 (Establishment, etc. of Association)

(1) Housing managers, etc. may establish an association of housing managers to efficiently conduct research on technical, administrative and legal matters concerning managing multi-family housing and its affairs.

(2) Deleted. *<by Act No. 13805, Jan. 19, 2016>*

(3) An association (hereinafter referred to as the "Association") under paragraph (1) shall be a corporation. *<Amended by Act No. 13805, Jan. 19, 2016>*

(4) The Association shall be formed by registering the establishment thereof at the location of its principal office.

(5) The rights and duties of a member of the Association subjected to suspension of business and qualification by the Minister of Land, Infrastructure and Transport, the Mayor/Do Governor or the Mayor of a large city pursuant to this Act shall be suspended during a period for the suspension of his/her business and qualification, and where his/her qualification as a housing manager is revoked, he/she shall become disqualified as a member of the Association. *<Amended by Act No. 13805, Jan. 19, 2016>*

(6) Where housing managers intend to establish the Association, they shall prepare the articles of incorporation with the number of promoters under the following classification and pass a resolution in favor of the articles of incorporation at the inaugural general meeting, and obtain approval from the Minister of Land, Infrastructure and Transport. The foregoing shall also apply where it makes any alterations to the approved articles of incorporation:

1. Organization of housing managers: At least one-fifth of housing managers assigned to the head of the management office of multi-family housing;
2. Deleted. *<by Act No. 13805, Jan. 19, 2016>*

(7) Where the Minister of Land, Infrastructure and Transport grants approval under paragraph (6), he/she shall immediately officially announce the approval of the articles of incorporation.

Article 82 (Mutual Aid Program)

(1) The organization of housing managers (hereafter in this Article, referred to as

"organization of housing managers") under Article 81 (1) may operate a mutual aid program to indemnify the head of the management office from liability for damages under Article 66, to cover losses due to human and physical accidents that occur in multi-family housing, and to indemnify workers and business operators related to affairs concerning multi-family housing management from liability for damages. *<Amended by Act No. 14709, Mar. 21, 2017>*

(2) Where the organization of housing managers intends to operate a mutual aid program under paragraph (1), it shall enact the regulations governing a mutual aid program and obtain approval from the Minister of Land, Infrastructure and Transport. The foregoing shall also apply where it intends to amend the regulations governing a mutual aid program.

(3) The regulations governing a mutual aid program under paragraph (2) shall include matters necessary to operate the mutual aid program, such as the scope of the mutual aid program, the details of a mutual aid agreement, a mutual aid fund, mutual aid fees, accounting standards and the rate of accumulation of liability reserves, as prescribed by Presidential Decree.

(4) The organization of housing managers shall manage the accounting of a mutual aid program as a separate account by dividing it from other accounts, and where it intends to use liability reserves for other purposes, it shall obtain approval from the Minister of Land, Infrastructure and Transport.

(5) The organization of housing managers shall publicly notify the result of the yearly operation of a mutual aid program to members of the mutual aid program through a daily newspaper or its public relations magazine, as prescribed by Presidential Decree.

(6) Where the Minister of Land, Infrastructure and Transport deems that the organization of housing managers is likely to compromise the soundness of a mutual aid program because it fails to comply with this Act and/or the regulations governing a mutual aid program, he/she shall order it to take corrective action.

(7) Where the Minister of Land, Infrastructure and Transport makes a request, the Governor of the Financial Supervisory Service under the Act on the Establishment, etc. of Financial Services Commission may examine the mutual aid program of the organization of housing managers.

Article 83 (Guidance and Oversight of Association)

The Minister of Land, Infrastructure and Transport shall guide and oversee the Association.

Article 84 (Application Mutatis Mutandis of Civil Act)

Except as otherwise expressly provided for in this Act, the provisions concerning an incorporated association of the Civil Act shall apply mutatis mutandis to the Association.

Article 85 (Provision of Subsidies of Management Expenses)

(1) The head of a local government may subsidize some of the expenses incurred in managing multi-family housing, as prescribed by Ordinance of such local government. *<Amended by Act No. 13676, Dec. 29, 2015>*

(2) The State may finance some of the expenses incurred in maintaining, repairing and improving multi-family housing from the Housing and Urban Fund. *<Newly Inserted by Act No. 13676, Dec. 29, 2015>*

Article 86 (Organization Supporting Management of Multi-Family Housing)

(1) The Minister of Land, Infrastructure and Transport may designate and announce an institution or organization to conduct the following affairs as an organization supporting the management of multi-family housing (hereafter in this Article, referred to as "organization supporting the management of multi-family housing"):

1. Consultation about civil affairs and education related to the management of multi-family housing;
2. Support for the enactment and amendment of the management rules;
3. Support related to the composition and operation of the council of occupants' representatives;
4. Support for the formulation and adjustment of a long-term repair plan or technical support, such as advice and suggestions on the feasibility of construction works or

services;

5. Examination of and support for the management conditions of multi-family housing;
6. Support for the revitalization of the community of occupants, etc. of multi-family housing;
7. Support for examination, inspection and mediation of disputes of multi-family housing;
8. Research and study into the status of the management of multi-family housing;
9. Affairs requested or entrusted by the Minister of Land, Infrastructure and Transport or the head of a local government;
10. Other affairs prescribed by Presidential Decree for the protection of the rights and interests of occupants, etc. of multi-family housing and the transparency and efficiency of the management of multi-family housing.

(2) The Minister of Land, Infrastructure and Transport may fund or subsidize expenses incurred in operating an organization supporting the management of multi-family housing and conducting its affairs within the budget.

(3) An organization supporting the management of multi-family housing may recover all or some of the expenses incurred in conducting affairs under the subparagraphs of paragraph (1) from the management entity or the council of occupants' representatives.

Article 87 (Selection of Outstanding Management Complex of Multi - Family Housing)

(1) The Mayor/Do Governor may select exemplary management complexes of multi-family housing every year to encourage exemplary management of multi-family housing.

(2) The Minister of Land, Infrastructure and Transport may select, officially commend or pay prize money to outstanding management complexes of multi-family housing among exemplary management complexes of multi-family housing selected by Mayors/Do Governors pursuant to paragraph (1), and provide other necessary support.

(3) Necessary matters concerning selecting exemplary management complexes of multi-family housing and outstanding management complexes of multi-family housing, official commendation, the payment of prize money, etc. shall be prescribed and announced by the Minister of Land, Infrastructure and Transport.

Article 88 (Establishment, Operation, etc. of Multi - Family Housing Management Information System)

(1) The Minister of Land, Infrastructure and Transport may establish and operate a multi-family housing management information system through which information on the management of multi-family housing may be comprehensively managed to improve transparency and efficiency in the management of multi-family housing, and provide related institutions, organizations, etc. with information thereon.

(2) The Minister of Land, Infrastructure and Transport may request related institutions, organizations, etc. to provide data necessary for establishing and operating a multi-family housing management information system under paragraph (1). In such cases, related institutions, organizations, etc. shall comply with such request except in extenuating circumstances.

(3) Mayors/Do Governors may comprehensively manage information on the management of multi-family housing, and provide related institutions, organizations, etc. with information thereon or request them to provide information thereon. In such cases, related institutions, organizations, etc. shall comply with such request except in extenuating circumstances.

Article 89 (Delegation and Entrustment of Authority)

(1) The Minister of Land, Infrastructure and Transport may delegate part of his/her authority under this Act to Mayors/Do Governors or the head of an agency under the jurisdiction of the Ministry of Land, Infrastructure and Transport, as prescribed by Presidential Decree.

(2) The Minister of Land, Infrastructure and Transport or the head of a local government may entrust the following authority among the authority under this Act to persons

recognized by him/her among corporations established for the purpose of the specialization of the management of multi-family housing, the safety management of structures, the certification of qualification, etc., as prescribed by Presidential Decree:

1. Education of members of the council of occupants' representatives under Article 17;
2. Education on the adjustment of a long-term repair plan under Article 29;
3. Crime prevention education, safety education on firefighting, safety education on structures under Article 32;
4. Safety management of small-scale multi-family housing under Article 34;
5. Receipt of the details of assignment to the head of the management office and a report of an official seal under Article 64 (5);
6. Implementation of qualifying examinations for probationary housing managers under Article 67 (1);
7. Education of housing management service providers and the heads of the management offices under Article 70;
8. Establishment and operation of a multi-family housing management information system under Article 88 (1).

Article 90 (Prohibition, etc. against Performing Unlawful Acts)

(1) The council of occupants' representatives (including its members; hereafter in this Article, the same shall apply) and the head of the management office shall not conspire together to unlawfully acquire or provide a fortune or property benefits in relation to the management of multi-family housing.

(2) Occupants, etc., the management entity, the council of occupants' representatives and the election committee (including its members) shall not unlawfully acquire or provide a monetary or other financial benefits in relation to the management of multi-family housing.

(3) The council of occupants' representatives and the management entity shall not use management expenses, user fees and reserves for long-term repairs other than the purposes under this Act.

(4) No housing management service provider, housing manager, etc. shall require other persons to conduct business or affairs under this Act using his/her name or trade name, or lend his/her registration certificate or qualification certificate to other persons. *<Amended by Act No. 13805, Jan. 19, 2016>*

Article 91 (Compulsory Collection of Unpaid Reserves for Long-Term Repairs)

Where reserves for long-term repairs or management expenses managed by the management entity that is the State or a local government are unpaid, the State or a local government may compulsorily collect the relevant reserves for long-term repairs or management expenses, in the same manner as unpaid national taxes or local taxes are collected.

Article 92 (Reports, Examinations, etc.)

(1) Where the Minister of Land, Infrastructure and Transport or the head of a local government deems it necessary, he/she may require a person who has obtained permission, made a report, or registered pursuant to this Act to make a necessary report, or a relevant public official to have access to a place of business and conduct necessary examinations.

(2) Where a public official conducts an examination under paragraph (1), he/she shall notify a person who is due to undergo an examination of an examination plan, such as the date and time of the examination, grounds for examination, and the details of the examination, seven days prior to the examination: Provided, That the foregoing shall not apply to urgent cases or where he/she deems that it is impossible to attain the purpose of the examination due to the destruction of evidence, etc. if he/she gives prior notice.

(3) A public official who conducts an examination pursuant to paragraph (1) shall carry a certificate of identification indicating his/her authority and produce such certificate to the relevant persons.

Article 93 (Oversight of Management of Multi-Family Housing)

(1) In any of the following cases, the head of a local government may require occupants, etc., the council of occupants' representatives or its members, the

management entity, or the election committee or its members to report matters concerning affairs prescribed by Presidential Decree, such as the details, etc. of the use of management expenses, or to submit data, or issue other necessary orders thereto, and require public officials under his/her jurisdiction to have access to the place of business, the management office, etc. and examine or inspect facilities, books, documents, etc. of multi-family housing for the efficiency of the management of multi-family housing and the protection of occupants, etc. In such cases, public officials who have access and conduct examinations shall carry a certificate of identification indicating his/her authority and produce such certificate to the relevant persons: *<Amended by Act No. 13786, Jan. 19, 2016; Act No. 14709, Mar. 21, 2017>*

1. Where it is necessary to conduct an audit under paragraph (3) or (4);
2. Where it is necessary to take measures because the aforesaid persons violate this Act or orders or dispositions under this Act;
3. Where it is necessary to mediate a dispute within a multi-family housing complex;
4. Where it is necessary for the safety management of structures of multi-family housing;
5. Where the council of occupants' representatives, etc. violates any of the management rules of multi-family housing;
6. Where it is necessary to oversee the management of multi-family housing.

(2) In cases falling under paragraph (1) 2, 3 or 5, occupants, etc. of multi-family housing may request the head of a local government to conduct an inspection of affairs of the council of occupants' representatives or its members, the management entity, the head of the management office, or the election committee or its members with the consent of at least three-tenths of all occupants, etc. In such cases, such occupants, etc. shall request inspection in writing, stating grounds therefor, and include information supporting such rounds.

(3) Where the head of a local government deems that a request for inspection under paragraph (2) is reasonable, he/she shall conduct an inspection and notify occupants, etc. who have requested for inspection of the result thereof.

(4) Where the head of a local government deems an inspection necessary for the efficiency of the management of multi-family housing and the protection of occupants, etc. even if no inspection is required under paragraph (2), he/she may conduct an inspection of affairs subject to inspection under paragraph (2).

(5) Where the head of a local government conducts an inspection pursuant to paragraph (3) or (4), he/she may seek advice from an expert, such as an attorney-at-law or a certified public accountant, or inspect the place of business, the management office, etc. together with the relevant expert.

(6) Matters necessary to request and conduct inspections under paragraphs (2) through (5) shall be prescribed by municipal ordinance of a local government.

Article 93-2 (Establishment, etc. of Complaint Center of Irregularities in Management of Multi-Family Housing)

(1) The Minister of Land, Infrastructure and Transport may establish and operate the Complaint Center of Irregularities in the Management of Multi-family Housing (hereinafter referred to as the "Complaint Center") to efficiently conduct affairs concerning the receipt, handling, etc,. of reports on unlawful acts related to irregularities in the management of multi-family housing.

(2) The Complaint Center shall conduct the following affairs:

1. Consultation about and receipt of reports related to unlawful acts in the management of multi-family housing;
2. Requesting the head of the relevant local government to examine the relevant matters reported and to take measures;
3. Notifying a reporter of a summary of the results of the examination and measures taken.

(3) A person who recognizes an unlawful act in relation to the management of multi-family housing may report such unlawful act to the Complaint Center. In such cases, a person who intends to file a report shall submit the details of such unlawful act, evidence, etc. to the Complaint Center along with documents in which he/she

mentions his/her personal details, the purport of, reasons for and details of the report and to which he/she affixes his/her signature.

(4) The head of a local government who receives a request under paragraph (2) 2 shall promptly complete an examination and take measures based on the relevant request, and notify the Minister of Land, Infrastructure and Transport of the results thereof within ten days from the date he/she completes the examination and takes measures, and where the Minister of Land, Infrastructure and Transport receives the notification thereof, he/she shall immediately notify a reporter of a summary of the results thereof.

(5) In addition to matters provided for in paragraphs (1) through (4), necessary matters concerning the establishment, operation and affairs of the Complaint Center, reporting and handling of irregularities, etc. shall be prescribed by Presidential Decree.

[This Article Newly Inserted by Act No. 14793, Apr. 18, 2017]

Article 94 (Suspension etc. of Construction Works)

Where the business entity, etc. occupants, etc. of multi-family housing, the management entity, the council of occupants' representatives or its members violate(s) this Act and/or an order issued or measure taken under this Act, the Minister of Land, Infrastructure and Transport or the head of a local government may order it or them to suspend construction works, make restoration to its original state, perform repairs of defects or take other necessary measures. *<Amended by Act No. 14793, Apr. 18, 2017>*

Article 95 (Hearings)

Where the Minister of Land, Infrastructure and Transport or the head of a local government intends to take measures falling under any of the following, he/she shall hold hearings:

1. Revoking permission to engage in an activity under Article 35 (5);
2. Canceling the registration of housing management services under Article 53 (1);
3. Deleted. *<by Act No. 13805, Jan. 19, 2016>*
4. Revoking qualification of a housing manager, etc. under Article 69 (1).

Article 96 (Legal Fiction as Public Officials in Applying Penalty Provisions)

Where the provisions of Articles 129 through 132 of the Criminal Act apply, any of the following persons shall be deemed a public official:

1. A member of the Defect Dispute Mediation Committee under Article 40 (1) or an employee of the Secretariat of the Defect Dispute Mediation Committee, who is not a public official;
2. A person who inspects of defects pursuant to Article 48 (1);
3. A person who is a member of the Multi-family Housing Management Dispute Mediation Committee under Article 71 (1) or an employee of the Secretariat of the Central Dispute Mediation Committee, who is not a public official.

Article 97 (Penalty Provisions)

Any person who unlawfully acquires or provides a monetary or other financial benefits in conspiracy with other persons in violation of Article 90 (1) shall be punished by imprisonment with prison labor for not more than three years or by a fine of not exceeding 30 million won: Provided, That a person in whose case an amount equivalent to 50 percent of a profit he/she has made from such violation exceeds 30 million won shall be punished by imprisonment with prison labor for not more than three years or by a fine of not exceeding an amount equivalent to double the profit.

Article 98 (Penalty Provisions)

Any of the following persons shall be punished by imprisonment with prison labor for not more than two years or by a fine of not exceeding 20 million won: Provided, That a person who falls under subparagraph 3, in whose case an amount equivalent to 50 percent of a profit he/she has made from such violation exceeds 20 million won shall be punished by imprisonment with prison labor for not more than two years or by a fine of not exceeding an amount equivalent to double the profit:

1. A person who provides housing management services without obtaining registration under Article 52 (1) or a person who obtains registration by fraud or other improper means;

2. Deleted; *<by Act No. 13805, Jan. 19, 2016>*
3. A person who unlawfully acquires or provides a monetary or other financial benefits in violation of Article 90 (2).

Article 99 (Penalty Provisions)

Any of the following persons shall be punished by imprisonment with prison labor for not more than one year or by a fine of not exceeding 10 million won: *<Amended by Act No. 14709, Mar. 21, 2017>*

1. A person who fails to undergo an audit or undergoes an audit by fraudulent means, in violation of Article 26 (1) and (2);

1-2. A person who performs acts falling under any of the subparagraphs of Article 26 (5), such as interfering with an audit, in violation of Article 26 (5);

1-3. A person who fails to prepare or keep books and documentary evidence, or prepares or keeps false books and documentary evidence, in violation of Article 27 (1);

1-4. A person who violates Article 35 (1) and (3) (excluding a person who engages in an activity without reporting the activities subject to reporting among activities under the subparagraphs of paragraph (1) of the aforesaid Article);

2. A person who divulges confidential information he/she has became aware of in the course of performing in violation of Articles 50 (2) and 78;
3. A person who conducts business during a period for suspension of business under Article 53 or conducts business after the registration of housing management services has been cancelled;
4. Deleted.; *<by Act No. 13805, Jan. 19, 2016>*
5. A person who performs duties of the head of the management office without obtaining qualification of housing manager, etc. pursuant to Article 67 or a person who allows a person not qualified to perform duties of the head of the management office;
6. A person who lends his/her registration certificate or qualification certificate in violation of Article 90 (4);
7. A person who refuses, interferes with or evades an examination or inspection under Article 92 (1) or 93 (1), (3) or (4);
8. A person who violates an order to suspend construction works under Article 94.

Article 100 (Penalty Provisions)

Any of the following persons shall be punished by a fine not exceeding ten million won:

1. A person who provides management services without having technical human resources or equipment under Article 6 (1);
2. A person who fails to assign a housing manager, etc. in violation of Article 64 (1).

Article 101 (Joint Penalty Provisions)

Where the representative of a corporation, or an agent, or employee of or other persons employed by a corporation or an individual commits an offense falling under any of Articles 97 through 99 in relation to affairs of such corporation or individual, not only shall the person who commits such offense be punished but such corporation or individual also shall be punished by a fine under the relevant provisions: Provided, That the foregoing shall not apply where the corporation or the individual has not neglected to pay due attention to or exercise reasonable supervision over the relevant affairs to prevent such offense.

Article 102 (Administrative Fines)

(1) Any person who uses a security deposit for repairing defects other than the purposes under this Act in violation of Article 38 (2) shall be punished by an administrative fine of not exceeding 20 million won.

(2) Any of the following persons shall be punished by an administrative fine of not exceeding ten million won: *<Amended by Act No. 13805, Jan. 19, 2016>*

1. A person who fails to transfer affairs concerning the management of multi-family housing in violation of Article 13;
2. and 3. Deleted; *<by Act No. 14709, Mar. 21, 2017>*
4. A person who fails to replace or repair important facilities in accordance with a

formulated or adjusted long-term repair plan in violation of Article 29 (2);
5. A person who fails to repair any defects discovered pursuant to Article 43 (3);
6. A person who uses a similar name in violation of Article 52 (5);
7. A person who violates an order to make a report or submit data under Article 93 (1);
8. A person who dismisses the head of the management office or requests a housing management service provider to dismiss him/her in violation of Article 65 (5);
9. A person who uses management expenses, user fees and reserves for long-term repairs for purposes other than the purposes under this Act in violation of Article 90 (3).

(3) Any of the following persons shall be punished by an administrative fine of not exceeding five million won: *<Amended by Act No. 13676, Dec. 29, 2015; Act No. 13786, Jan. 19, 2016; Act No. 14793, Apr. 18, 2017>*
1. A person who fails to organize an autonomous management body under Article 6 (1);
2. A person who selects a housing management service provider in violation of Article 7 (1) or business operator in violation of Article 25;
3. A person who fails to report a determination as to and an alteration to the methods of management, the enactment and amendment of the management rules, the composition and alteration of the council of occupants' representatives under Articles 11 (3) and 19;
4. A person who fails to prepare the minutes, require the management entity to keep the minutes, or comply with a request for perusal or reproduction of the minutes in violation of Article 14 (6);
5. A person who fails to disclose the details of management expenses, etc. in violation of Articles 23 (4), or makes a false disclosure;
6. A person who fails to report or disclose the results of an audit in violation of Article 26 (3), or make a false report or disclosure;
7. Deleted; *<by Act No. 14709, Mar. 21, 2017>*
8. A person who fails to comply with a request for perusal or reproduction of information, such as books or evidential documents, in violation of Article 27 (2), or provides false information in response to such request;
9. A person who fails to disclose a written contract in violation of Article 28, or discloses a false written contract;
10. A person who fails to formulate or examine a long-term repair plan or to record or keep matters examined concerning a long-term repair plan in violation of Article 29;
11. A person who fails to accumulate reserves for long-term repairs under Article 30;
12. A person who fails to keep design documents, etc. or to record, keep and maintain the details of the replacement, repair, etc. of facilities pursuant to Article 31;
13. A person who fails to formulate or implement a safety management plan under Article 32 or to undergo safety education;
14. A person who fails to conduct safety inspections pursuant to Article 33 (1) or to give notification or make a report to the council of occupants' representatives or the head of a Si/Gun/Gu or to take necessary measures pursuant to paragraph (2) of the aforesaid Article;
15. A person who engage in any activities under the subparagraphs of Article 35 (1) without reporting;

15-2. A person who fails to comply with an order to take corrective action on the repair of defects under Article 37 (4);

16. A person who fails to make a report under Article 38 (2), or make a false report;

16-2. A safety inspection agency or a relevant expert that fails to comply with a request for attendance at a meeting made by the Defect Dispute Mediation Committee, in violation of Article 43 (6);

17. A person who fails to submit a written reply to mediation, etc. under Article 46 (2) to the Defect Dispute Mediation Committee or a person who fails to submit a

written reply to an application for mediation of a dispute under Article 75 (1) to the Central Dispute Mediation Committee;

18. A person who fails to respond in mediation, etc. under Article 46 (3) (excluding occupants and lessees) or a person who fails to respond to mediation of a dispute under Article 75 (2);

18-2. A person who refuses or interferes with an examination, inspection and perusal under Article 51 (1);

19. A person who fails to report any alterations to matters in the registration of housing management services under Article 52 (1) or makes a false report;

20. and 21. Deleted; *<by Act No. 13805, Jan. 19, 2016>*

22. A person who manages multi-family housing in violation of Article 63 (2);

23. A person who fails to report the details of assignment, an official seal or any alterations under Article 64 (5);

24. A person who fails to submit a document proving the fact that he/she has subscribed to guarantee insurance, etc. under Article 66 (3);

25. A person who fails to undergo education under Article 70;

26. A person who violates an order to make a report or an inspection under Article 92 (1).

(4) The Minister of Land, Infrastructure and Transport or the head of a local government shall impose administrative fines under the provisions of paragraphs (1) through (3), as prescribed by Presidential Decree.

Index

Editor

Korea Research Institute of Housing Management
(Website: www.krihm.org)

The Korea Research Institute of Housing Management (KRIHM) was established in 2013 in order to build a systematic housing management system that can adapt to the change of focus from construction and supply to maintenance and management, and to contribute to advanced and specialized management and institutional development based on academic and practical research on housing management. KRIHM is a research institute that identifies problems in the housing management system, explores alternatives, and pursues the direction for future development through in-depth discussions. KRIHM conducted research such as The Nature of Multi-Family Housing Management and Trend Analysis of Management Expenses (2013), Guidelines of Multi-Family Housing Management for Improving the Expertise of Resident (2014), Working Environment Survey for Workers Engaged in Multi-Family Housing Management (2015), A Study on the Direction of Development in the Multi-Family Housing Management System (2016), and A Study on Measures to Improve the Quality of Housing Management Service System (2017). It published books including *Contemporary Multifamily Housing Management: Theory and Practice* (2014), *A New Paradigm for Multifamily Housing Management* (2016), *The Reality of Apartment Workers: Can We Work Happily?* (2017), and *Community in Multi-Family Housing Complex* (2017). It also held academic seminars including Innovate the Paradigm of Multi-Family Housing Management (2018) and Long-term Repair Plan for Multi-Family Housing: Current Status of Legislation and Major Issues (2018).

Contributors

Seong-Kyu Ha
Seong-Kyu Ha is an Emeritus Professor of Urban Planning and Real Estate at Chung-Ang University, South Korea. He also serves as the president of the Korea Research Institute of Housing Management. He received his Ph.D. in Urban Planning from University College London and an MSc from the London School of Economics. His current research interests have centered on low-income housing policies, urban residential regeneration and housing management. He has authored numerous publications on housing policy and urban and community regeneration, including Housing Policy, Wellbeing and Social Development in Asia (with Rebecca L. H. Chiu, Routledge, 2018). Recently, he was elected Chairman of the Korea Housing Service Society, a housing expert consulting and research group in Korea. He is on the Board of Directors of the Korea Land and Housing Corporation.

Kwan-Ho Myong
After passing the Judicial Examination, Kwan-Ho Myong received training at the Judicial Research and Training Institute (2010, 39th graduating class). He worked in law firms including Lee & Ko, handling lawsuits and providing consultations in various areas such

as civil and criminal cases and administrative affairs. He serves as the Legal Affairs Officer at the Korea Housing Managers Association.

Ah-Rim Ahn

Ah-Rim Ahn graduated from the Department of Urban Planning and Real Estate at Chung-Ang University, and received a Ph.D. in Urban Planning from the graduate school of the same university. Currently, Ahn works for the Korea Research Institute of Housing Management. Ahn received her Ph.D. with a dissertation titled A Study on Effects of Regional Income Level on Subjective Income Status, and impact on Subjective Well-being-Focused on Reference Group Effects (2017). Currently, she is conducting research on the multi-family housing management system and residential satisfaction.

Eun-Taek Kang

Eun-Taek Kang received a Ph.D. in Urban Planning from the Department of Urban Planning and Real Estate at Chung-Ang University, and currently works for the Korea Research Institute of Housing Management. Kang's major research achievements include A Study on the Factors Affecting Household Choices of Dwelling: Focused on the Characteristics of Home Owning Renters (2008), A Study on the Factors Affecting the Time to Purchase a Home for The First Time-Focused on Survival Analysis (2011), Intergenerational Effects of Parental Wealth on Children's Housing Wealth (2015), Migration Behavior of Students and Graduates Under Prevailing Regional Dualism: The Case of South Korea (2017), etc. Currently, he is conducting research on housing policy, housing management system, and housing relocation.

Ta-Kwan Choi

As a housing manager, Ta-Kwan Choi held the position of chief manager in charge of practical affairs in the field, working as the head of the management office and an executive of an entrusted management company for 22 years. Choi received a master's degree in engineering from the Graduate School of Housing at Seoul National University of Science and Technology, and a Ph.D. in Economics from the Graduate School of Energy and Environment at the same university, majoring in Building Energy Management. He was a co-author of study materials for the housing manager qualification exam, and participated in the publication of *Multi-Family Housing Management Practice* (2002). Currently, he serves as Vice President and Director of Planning and Coordination at the Korea Research Institute of Housing Management. As a housing management specialist, he is also dedicated to the research on the legislative system and the system's improvement, as well as teaching.

Byung-Nam Park

Byunng-Nam Park graduated from the Graduate School of Architectural Engineering at the University of Seoul and received a Ph.D. in Real Estate from Kangwon National University. Park is a member of the first graduating class of housing managers, and works as a manager of practical affairs in the field as a pioneer of the Korean housing management system. Currently, he serves as Secretary-General of the Korea Housing Managers Association, and supervises management offices across the nation. He is a specialist in multi-family housing management and the relevant legislative system. He is an adjunct professor at Kangwon National University and Myongji University.

Multi-Family Housing Management in Korea

First published 2019 by *parkyoungsa*

Editor	Korea Research Institute of Housing Management
Contributors	Seong-Kyu Ha · Kwan-Ho Myong · Ah-Rim Ahn · Eun-Taek Kang · Ta-kwan Choi · Byung-Nam Park
Publisher	Jong-Man Ahn · Sang-Jun Ahn
Publisher editor	Geun-Ha Bae
Marketing	Se-Gi Park
Cover illustration	A-Ra Jo
Printer	In-Do Woo · Cheol-Min Go

parkyoungsa

36, Saemunan-ro 3-gil, Jongno-gu, Seoul, Republic of Korea
1959. 3. 11. 300-1959-1.
tel (82) 2 733-6771 fax (82) 2 736-4818 e-mail pys@pybook.co.kr
homepage www.pybook.co.kr ISBN 979-11-303-0869-2 93350

13,000won